JOURNAL OF AN OLD HIPPIE CHICK
IN THE DESERT

with wonder dog Luna Luckdragon;
a memoir of poetry, free verse, journaling,
and indigenous tales

by

Terry M. Mandeville

This book is a memoir, journal, collection of poetry, and a work of nonfiction. It reflects the author's present recollections of experiences over time. In many instances, however, certain names, locations, identifying characteristics and details regarding people described in this book have been altered or combined to protect their anonymity. Some events have been compressed and combined, and some dialogue has been recreated.

Drawings and images by Terry M. Mandeville.

Printed in the United States of America

First printing edition 2024

TABLE OF CONTENTS

DEDICATION

Thank you to Luna Luckdragon for her unparalleled friendship, love, comfort, understanding, and sense of adventure; for this special connection between canine and human.

Thank you to my writing "tribes" for the opportunity, support, suggestions, encouragement, and tools; to the Women's Writing Groups, and all of the women there, for the support and the prompts that drew forth so many memories; to the Duvall Art Salon for listening and encouraging.

I am grateful for the sacred and inspiring writing spaces throughout Joshua Tree National Park; as well as many inspirational spaces encompassed within my homes away-from-home at Luna Mesa, Peaceful Vista Ranch, Sunshine for Your Soul, Sahara Madre, and Martian Rose.

fifth life

first growing
      becoming
perused by heady idealism
      ...what should be
      ...what is right
      ...what is moral

fade to finding a niche
      within what is
settle into complacency
      be old
            maybe not wise
      coast

now!
unclench
      breathe
            next is not to worry
      see
            without distraction
      time for wonderment
            time for peace
      time for self

INTRODUCTION

Terry M. Mandeville

winter at the lake

crisp cool the air in the woods there
evergreens tall
deep and quiet, silent
upward to the sky over all
majestic
reach up, up to mountain tops

winter rages
ancient seasonal changes
primeval metamorphosis
lost in time prehistoric

winter
bare trees between the green
cold and naked
the scene sacred

winter winds blow fierce, pierce the calm
no cover, heavy grey sky
snow comes right along
lake freezes over
and the swans fly and skate at their landing

It's raining. It's bone-soaking chilly. Before I can venture outside, I have to find my grey wooly socks, fluffy purple down jacket with the hood that my son gave me for my birthday, old scuffed water repellent boots, and brown Chateau Ste. Michelle Winery cap with the brim to keep the droplets off my face. The rain and the dampness seem to be getting under my skin now in a way they never did when I was younger. It's raining. Seems like it is always raining. Although I must admit it does make the sunshine all that more treasured, it has become so dreary and gloomy.

It's raining, and I feel tears coming. I don't really understand why. Irrational sadness. Situational depression flutters around my edges, pushes in when I least expect it. Seasonal Affective Disorder, the blues of winter, hits me every year now in the late fall. Listless, no energy, sleeping and eating too much.

My lake is beautiful. Peaceful and easy. In the summer it is filled with birds and life. Surrounded by green, emerald green like no other. It quiets my mind and brings a never-ending source of joy and entertainment.

On the other hand, in the winter the rains come hard. Non-stop. Drops drum a rhythm on my roof. Rivulets carve out the driveway. Algae and moss grow on the fences, pathways, tree trunks and walls of the houses. Everything outside is wet, muddy, slimy and green. Everything inside is damp. Bread molds within a day or two on the counter. Salt and spices cake up in their containers. The river by town rises and floods the farmlands. Roads become impassible one by one and the town almost becomes an island.

Then the wind. It starts with ripples on the water and waving branches of the alder trees. Next the firs start to sway and white caps form on the lake. A few times a year the storms rev up big time. The roots of the trees desperately try to hold on to saturated ground, some let go and topple across power lines and roads. Electricity can be knocked out for days.

Finally, the cold. It snows up at my lake when all below is still raining. The lake freezes over; not in that fun way that allows skating or ice fishing. Feet of snow cover my long steep driveway and the road around the lake. Plowing and sanding this road is low priority for the county. Generators go on, not forever as the fuel runs out. Wood stoves and fireplaces burn. Everyone hunkers down. All is quiet and isolated.

In the beginning this is all a grand adventure, a lark, especially the snow. Real seasons, not experienced at the lower elevations in my neck of the woods. Beautiful and pure, decorating the Douglas Fir and covering the ground. Swans fly in with huge wings and skid on the ice, ducks find little pockets to swim near the inlet. Quiet permeates. A fire in the fireplace, crackling, fills the air with age-old scent.

As I get older, the obnoxious sound and smell of neighboring generators begins to wear on me. I am sick of being wet and cold. Sick of parking the truck at the top of the driveway so I can get out. Sick of sliding off the hairpin turn on the way to town.

Driving down the winding road, and through the valley, I feel a heavy sadness. Stark bare limbs crowd the hillside. Grey sky presses down. I cross the bridge, tunneling under the rain forest branches of moss dripping moisture. Dampness gets deep into my bones. I feel a chill and hint of refracted light in the dark clouds above. It's going to snow tonight.

I love the Pacific Northwest foothills; the deep greens of the trees and groundcover, the rich smells of moist earth, the cool water. I must say, however, that at some point these winters have become a little difficult.

I need a change for a bit. I need to get out of here, hit the road. I need a new adventure. Something completely different for these elder years. A new chapter with goals to look forward to and to get my creative juices flowing again.

I was born in the Pacific Northwest. I grew up here and came to maturity during the '60s and '70s, a flower child of the era. In retrospect I guess I was what would have been called a "hippie" in those years, although that was not a term well-regarded by my peers at the time. Life did involve peace, love, drugs, rock and roll, communal living and free love for a while during that chapter of my life.

Journal Of An Old Hippie Chick In The Desert

Now I am in my 70s. I can't imagine how that could have come to pass, but it seems to be true. My kids are grown and embedded in their own journeys and phases of life. My life partner, Bob, died several years ago. I have lived in a little old house on the shores of a clear lake nestled in the foothills of the Cascade Mountains for more than a decade, recently joined by my canine companion, Luna Luckdragon. I moved here with Bob when he became too disabled to work anymore. After he passed, I stayed.

I had known that Bob was dying for quite a long time, and that I would be left alone. I found that the knowing of this fact, versus the actual anguish of going through it, is not the same thing at all. Death is undeniably not an event that one can truly prepare for. The delaminating and unravelling of us, into me again after 33 years, was such a very long journey. All of it, every inch, every new instance of loss was soul shattering. The slow demise of what we had was unstoppable. Intimacy vanished. My best friend was ebbing away. I watched the person that was Bob slowly fade, like a sunset. There were so many losses during his last years, primarily losing myself in the caring for the man every day and night, managing his pain and his growing dependency, and existing on fumes. Eventually he passed and I found myself drowning in ambivalence, while at the same time experiencing incapacitating grief. It took several years to soak it all in and for me to come alive again.

Now I am on my own. I am kind of amazed to realize, finally, that I have no one to be responsible to. No one to confer with before I go my own way, do my own thing. I have really never lived entirely by myself before, and find it quite a pleasant unfamiliarity to consider going off on an adventure on my own without consulting anyone. To do what I want without having to explain myself. To explore. To find my next path.

I have kept journals and written poetry of one kind or another through all phases of my life's journeys. I ache to begin a new journey now, along a course conducive to putting it all down on paper. I need a complete startle for the senses. I am aiming for clear skies where warm breezes caress to blow the cobwebs from my mind.

Journal Of An Old Hippie Chick In The Desert

The ability to take a journey in life does not need to end. The opportunities are endless, regenerated and renewed. My first journeys in life were those of growing and becoming my adult me. Then there were the journeys pursued by heady idealism: what should be, what was right, finding morality. Then I faded to finding a niche within what is, and more or less settling into complacency. That was the time when I kind of coasted along. It was not a bad thing. I paused, found calm and security, raised children.

Now is the time to unclench, breathe, see again without distraction. With any luck, there is plenty of time for peace before the final journey takes me into the unknown. Time for myself where words and poetry flow, deep emotions pour out, notions clarify and understanding blooms. This may be what is deemed a second childhood, perhaps. I am not sure. It seems to be a time to re-examine the truths and beliefs developed in my inspired earlier years. All those things that I put on the back burner for a bit. Busting through the excuses. No more "I will do it later." I am not "too busy." Hell, I have no obligations, no job, no one to take care of.

So much is behind me; so much growth and change. So many things weathered. So much time spent waiting for love, for independence, for time, for a family and then for the kids to grow up. I have been waiting for a quiet mind. Every time I seem to get a glimpse of the sky, it clouds up again. Every time the sun comes out, by the time I can turn my face upwind, here comes the rain again.

One day there will be no warning, no time to plan. One day I will just disappear and never get the chance back. I used to be known for my patience. It used to be my strength. Now, it seems, the reality is that I haven't got as much time to waste. There are beginnings ahead, like those before, giving hope and purpose.

Each place I have visited, every adventure I have taken, has its own path, its own value, its own journey if I just remain open to be shown the way. Sometimes I over-plan, too structured, and don't leave room to be led. Sometimes I am lazy and miss what I am destined to see. Perhaps I need to sit back and let the mystery unfold on its own this time.

Choosing what direction, where to go, is a dilemma. The infinite variety of our planet astounds me. I want a new experience that I can settle into for a bit, more than just a few days. To feel a part of something, understand the rhythms of a new place, be a native for a while, but not too long. Not so long that I get sad and yearn for home.

The mountains are beauty and inspiration. Snow, ice and cold streams reflect. Jagged spires reach up and rise towards the sun. Goats tread a path along cliff ledges. Fragrant pines cling to the craggy slopes. Marmots dance and bob in the rocks. The problem is that mountains are cold and I need warmth. No, mountains are not my destination this time.

Forests are enchantment with deep greens of hemlock and fir. Cedar and alder stand atop a bed of salal sprinkled with the dusty blue of Oregon Grape, the orange of salmonberry, red of thimbleberry. Shade covers soft mossy beds. Black bears look for elderberries and itch against sturdy tree trunks. Cougars lie among the rocks. Then again, forests are dark and I crave the sunlight. I will save the forests for another time.

Rivers lead onward; encompassing pools, eddies and rushing waters. They course and curve, continually etching a new path with waterfalls and oxbow lakes. Geese fly, steelhead flash silver. Rivers flood, however, and I need dryer lands. I will cross the rivers many times, but they are not my journey right now.

Oceans are the mother of creation; dark, inky and deep. I reflect upon the mighty pulsing roar of the ocean waves topped by white foam, cresting and falling over grey sand and rocks. I know the salt spray in the air, decaying seaweed on the shore, pebbles sanded smooth over billions of years and the rhythm of the waves. Salmon glide through the water and sea creatures slide along the blue-black deeps. Seagulls play in the wind. Then again, oceans are misty and stormy in winter and I require peace. I will wait for summer to visit the ocean.

Lakes sparkle like jewels in their variety in the forests, the valleys, the scablands, the farm country. There are reservoirs, little ponds, and huge lakes with no end in sight. Ancient land-locked remnants of seas are salty still. Ice cold blue mountain lakes are surrounded by meadows of pure white avalanche lily and bright purple-red Indian paintbrush. Mineral-rich pothole seep lakes are held in depressions of old lava. Rainbow trout leap to catch flies, eagles and hawks soar. Still, lakes freeze over and I need more heat. The lake will still be there when I return.

Valleys are cool and hidden. They wind down into concealed shady paradises of nettle and deer toed vanilla leaf. The deer seek the huckleberry. Tiny critters scurry and hide. Nevertheless, valleys are dank in winter and I need brightness. No, valleys are not my destination this time either.

Meadowlands are pastel beauty ablaze with alpine lily and lupine, encircled by fuzzy yellow bees. Elk graze. Meadows are in full glory in summer, but dormant in the winter and I need winter splendor. I will visit later when the flowers bloom.

Flat grasslands stretch for eternity. Dusty gold is punctuated by tumbleweed. Pronghorn, bison and wild horse roam. It is miles and miles with no people, no houses. Yet grasslands are barren and cold and I need beauty. I will not be venturing into the prairies this time.

Cities are a hustling heartbeat, noise on every corner, rushing people and cold hard concrete. Everywhere a purpose, a destination. Stray dogs scavenge, rats feed on garbage, pigeons peck at crumbs. Cities are unquestionably too busy. I need to encourage a quiet mind. No city for me for this adventure.

A few years ago, my older son and I went on an exploration of several national parks. When we got to the Mojave Desert, I found a completely new alien wonder. It was magical. It was breathtaking. It was surreal. It was sizzling hot in summer. At first glimpse it was merely rock, sand and dust with a lot of vacant dirt and scrub. Hidden within, however, was life of coyote and roadrunner, thorny cacti and sculpted rock. Then there were those twisted Joshua trees, all grotesque and graceful rolled into one. I was intrigued. One of those places where you say "someday I should come back here ...but maybe not in summer." Yes, I am thinking Joshua Tree, California might be the place, my sanctuary, the setting for this new journey.

I ask myself if I am really prepared to do this, or is it just a fantasy? A daydream? Am I all talk and no action? At 70-something am I too old?

To stay a couple of months I am going to need a car, transportation to get around, so I can't really fly down. Besides, I can't even begin to imagine Luna taking well to flying. Man, that is going to be one hell of a long drive, something like 1300 miles, not counting off highway meandering. Oh, I have done road trips before but usually with a human companion or two.

I am strong. I am smart. I am able to do this.

So, this is it! This will be my new adventure. My canine friend and I are off on a" Joshua Tree Sabbatical." A regeneration. A winding journey to a heretofore alien, amazing and extraordinary corner of the world.

Terry M. Mandeville

do it later

i need a change
do it later i say
i have all day
i want to stay still
i have no will to do it now

do it later
the young have forever, never questioning
always questing something more exciting

do it later
i cannot do it now
somehow something always gets in the way

do it later
time runs down
i don't know how
it seems now there is no time
to do it later

CHAPTER 1

ROAD TRIP

Luna, the little red truck, and I

Terry M. Mandeville

road trip

pack up the truck, grab the bedding
find the stove, don't know where we're heading

off the highway deserted roads
adventure finds us as it unfolds

it all awaits anytime, anywhere
just outside the fence, it's all there

take me on a dare
make me get up off this old chair

and go along the mountain trails
the city sidewalks, the road, the rails

the heat and cold, breathe the smell of the place
the colors, the feel, the pace

to go beyond what's known, to see it all
beyond the town, the river, beyond familiar walls

The new year has passed. May it be filled with peace, kindness, tolerance, love, and a little less senseless lunacy. Now, after the big celebratory sonic blasts of fireworks at the lake, I am hoping that I can peel Luna Luckdragon from under the bed by the time we head south for our two-month "sabbatical" in the desert. I will miss my Pacific Northwest friends, family and tribe, and the greens that surround me. Nevertheless, I am so looking forward to sun and the twisted Joshua trees.

Luna and I are venturing down to Joshua Tree, to the clear California desert. The loose plan is to plug away, camping or staying in little abodes and campgrounds along the way. We will marvel at all the scenery, dust and sand, oranges in winter, cacti, and Joshua trees.

I have this thick cushy old mattress in the back of my truck, and a lid over the truck bed. I can camp anywhere, crawl under my cozy quilt with my dog, and snuggle warm and dry. Best way ever to camp. Like a snail, carrying my home with me.

We take off south. After many goodbyes, dinners, and hopefully packing everything we need, Luna and I make it out the door at a reasonable time. Sky so clear that Mt. Rainier is out to observe our departure looking crystal sparkling white and majestic. As we mosey on, Mt. Baker is out too. I will miss their monolithic splendor watching over us.

We are not in a hurry, happy to take our time and do it slow. We will travel far, winding south, always south, through unfamiliar lands, amid strangers and a few strange ways. We are going my way, forever south.

I am lured by the idea of the coastal route, but winter is a time of high winds and landslides there and that part is not an adventure that appeals to me. Then again, I am enticed by the idea of the eastern high desert route with its scenic mountains, on the other hand winter is a time of bitter cold and piling snow at those elevations. So, the I-5 freeway it must be, with little parallel side jaunts as time and weather allow.

I realize that I have been living in the sticks far too long as I am entirely gob-smacked by the whizzing traffic, traffic, traffic everywhere on the freeway. Big trucks crowd. Zoom,

zoom. Little sports cars zip, weaving closely in and out of the lane, soon out of sight ahead.

Clouds start moving in as we head farther south. Grey cloudy skies lower to shroud the world around me. Deep greens, rich carpeted earth and moist air; rain spattered fields appear and pass. No change, no change. Miles chug by and still the rain. Wet pavement, yellow center lane, all the same, all the same.

By the time we hit Portland it's pouring rain so hard that I can barely see the car ahead of me. Windshield wipers flap back and forth on the high setting. Camping seems like a miserable idea. Just south of the city I see a Motel 6 sign blearily through the rain covered windshield and we pull in for the night. Storm's supposed to be in full swing by tomorrow.

Now, Motel 6s can be comfy or miserable, at a variable cost, but they all welcome dogs for no extra money. It is our go-to when all else fails. This one is not especially cheap and the small patch of grass for Luna's relief is unpleasant, completely covered with several layers of dog poop. However the room is warm and dry, and it has a bathtub. Well, the bathtub has seen better days, but it is a nice warm soak. Then we settle in to sleep, Luna taking up more than her share of the bed. Three o'clock in the morning I am awakened by water hitting my face and soaking my clothing on the floor. The ceiling sprinkler has sprung a leak. The desk clerk cannot fix it, accuses me of setting it off by smoking in the room (I quit smoking decades ago), and denies a refund or a new room. So, we are off in the wee hours amid the continuing storm as I compose an angry letter in my head to Motel 6.

Back on I-5 again we occasionally find a few spots to pull over and wait for windows to materialize through the backlash of the atmospheric river with its 50 mph gusts of wind and rain. A snack, get some coffee, try to walk the dog (who isn't willing at all to brave the storm).

Finally, we meander off the freeway around the Rogue River area. Churches and taverns come and go, just like in most small country towns. Little farms with chickens, goats and geese. We stop for an interlude, staying in a funky little cabin with a bunk bed, a table with one chair, a heater, one electrical outlet, and one old lamp. No TV, no internet, and very spotty cell phone reception, however it is an absolutely gorgeous setting along a river and waterfall, if it stops raining enough to see it. Beauty in the river and old man's beard hanging from the bare deciduous trees. Deer and wild turkey abound. Luna and I walk along the river in both directions, getting soaked each time. The rain and wind are not letting up. I sit at the rickety little table and do a little writing by the dim light. We would make a run for it when we could. We end up staying three nights.

When the chance finally comes, we do manage to start off again. The adventure of the Siskiyous leaving Oregon are a sudden change. Rain turns cold, and turns to snow as the road snakes around and over the passes into California. Climbing to new heights, then back down again. Dodging deluges of rain, snow and high wind gusts, winter sure can be an interesting time of year to road trip.

The mountains are hidden by low clouds. As we drive on past Mt. Shasta it is grey and miserable. We get no views of the mountain's splendor. We pull into a campground that is rather much still encased in snow and I pry my clenched fists from the steering wheel. It isn't snowing, or raining, at the moment, but it is really cold. I bundle in my down parka, hat, wool socks, and boots. Hmmm, seems familiar. Just like at home.

Luna's jacket is always a struggle since she seems to think it is a ridiculous thing. I manage to get it over her head and thread her paws through the leg holes. As it gets dark, I heat up the last of my fridge food from home on the camp stove, eat quickly, and crawl into the back of the truck, happy that we do not have to deal with being all wet from rain. Its early, but it's cold and dark, so we snuggle in under layers of quilt and sleeping bag. I am hoping I don't need to get up to pee in the middle of the night.

In the morning, we are off early again. We start driving in the dark and end in the dark. We are on the road early enough to see the sun rise, and late enough to see it set. We also see the full moon rise. All in one day! Miles tick away. Short stops for gas, pee breaks, dog walks, coffee, and food punctuate the drive.

Those first days of heavy rain have morphed to heavy fog. Encased in mist and haze, sightless, soundless, the journey continues. Then a little sun peeks out and quickly back to overcast and sprinkling. Then fog again. All the micro-clime pockets of California, each a different world.

'Long about Sacramento we peel off the freeway to highway 99 and push on along the Central Valley past unending lines of warehouses, truck stops, and strip malls all the way to Visalia at the edge of the Sequoias. A cute little bare-bones cabin awaits us at the KOA campground and we stay two nights.

Driving into Sequoia National Park we pay our respects to the massive ancient trees, although Luna is not a fan of the winding road up into the park. I find an easy trail amid the giants to walk off my stiff old legs and some of the other effects of sedentary driving. Then I go off to find good food and a beer in town. Luna and I chill at the cabin and rest our travel-worn bodies for a bit.

When it is time to leave, we are rested and ready. Back again to the endless agricultural backdrop. The endless pavement of the highway. Warehouses, one after another, like dominoes lining the way.

I have loaded my music on my tablet but I always have trouble figuring out how to connect and play it in the truck. Radio only plays religious music, extreme political banter, and the occasional Spanish-speaking stations. Wish I had taken Spanish in high school, it would have been way more useful than French in the places I frequent. Now the religious and political radio stations seem packed with doom and gloom, and that is kind of what I am trying to get away from. So, we happily listen to mariachi music and news in Spanish and I am amazed at how much Spanish I actually do recognize as I get older, how close some words are to English, and how much I have picked up at Ixtapa, my favorite Mexican restaurant back home.

Looking for a gas station, I leave the cluster of traffic, fill the tank and walk the dog. Then south, south, onward south. The world seems a foggy bog for all I can tell. At least it is no longer raining. The world is no longer flooding, no longer drowning me. Where is my clear blue sky?

Extraordinarily, through the fog, orchards appear. Trees with bright yellow shaped ornaments. Lemons! Trees with bright orange balls. Oranges! Incredible, oranges and lemons growing in the dead of winter! Bright and happy amid bleak surroundings. The faint citrus scent wafts towards me, tickles my nose and makes me happy.

We turn off highway 99, up the rolling hills. Through foggy forests of almond and olive, stretches of dusty earth and palm trees. Just past Tehachapi, suddenly, it seems to lighten a bit more. Am I imagining it? Is it real? Yes! We emerge from the fog. Out of the mist, to the right of the mist, rising out of the mist – a sole, solitary statue. A welcoming vanguard awaiting us, as we have been awaiting her. A Joshua tree!

I seem to have tears at the sight. We have at last entered the Mojave. Joshua trees! Scrawny little things in these parts, and not looking too healthy. I find myself both crying and laughing.

Terry M. Mandeville

Wide open, the road stretches like an old scar between hills and scant vegetation. We putt along, Luna and I, agog at the universe spread out before us like a tapestry of gold. Dust caked UPS trucks, cattle driving cowboys, wide open scrubland ringed by distant mountains and their snow patches. The golds of grasses, reds of budding twigs, whites of the minerals. Blackened trees and soil where fires have swept through. Glacial sculpted world. Bulls fight. Deer feed with the cows. Hawks soar, staying motionless, hovering in place in the wind. Expanses of quiet nothingness.

Little towns pop up; a weather-beaten café, abandoned gas station, smashed windows in the shell of an old trailer. Who has lived here? What did they do? Why did they leave?

I know I am close as we turn onto Old Woman Springs Road, named either for the old native women who lived here centuries ago while the rest of their tribe journeyed out to hunt, or for the outline of an old woman in the rocks, depending on which story you listen to. I know I am close as more communities pop up. Tiny colorful houses, mobile home parks, houses of stucco and tiled roofs, yards littered with old car parts, signs for sacred metaphysical services. Tattered old plastic bags are plastered by the wind to fences, no underbrush to hide them.

I know I am close as I hit the hill down, down, and finally I see the valley, our home for the next two months.

Terry M. Mandeville

heading south

heading south
no question
the direction

heading south
towards longer days
clearer skies
and sunshine rays

trucking on again
go we must
where the wind blows us
alongside the dust

CHAPTER 2

DESERT MOSAIC

can't hide in the desert

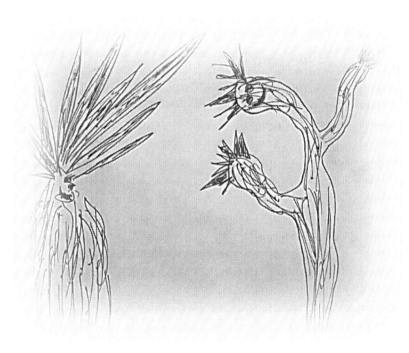

Terry M. Mandeville

you can't hide in the desert

here i am

feet firmly embedded in the golden sand
you can't hide in these desert lands

come a thousand miles
this flowerchild
self-exiled for a while
for a change, a trial
now completely beguiled
you can't hide in this wild

here sands lay bare
under sun's intense glare
the bright parched air
exposes the broken and in need of repair
you can't hide in the desert grandeur

deafening silence astounds
wide open surrounds
no rustling trees around
muzzled silence, only occasional muffled sounds
you just can't hide in the desert that has no bounds

feel the stress drain, flow
head to toe
flush into the desert slow
overflow
no trying to hide in the desert below

breathe deep
calmness seeps
creeps
sweeps you can't hide in the desert, you can only weep

tranquil to every pore
every crevice, every shore
muscles unknot to my very core
that i cannot hide in the desert i cannot ignore

the magical desert heals
away the trivial peels
gone is the unreal
leaving me with peace to feel
safe, easy, comfortable, ideal
no place to hide in the desert or to conceal

it begins to feel like home
by myself, but with my dog i am not alone
and i don't want to hide in this desert on my own

A new year, and I am really here! We have actually done it, Luna and I! It is not a dream, not just an idle idea. It is real! The Mojave Desert surrounds us amid the Joshua trees, wide open skies, and sand. This desert has been waiting for me, patiently and consistently.

We settle into our little home of the next couple of months, exploring and getting to know it, taking some time to make it our own. It is set on a rise above the village and has a breathtaking view of the hills and mountains in all directions, capturing the varying phases of the day and night. There is fenced in acreage and sand for Luna to run about, lots of little creatures for her to chase, and a Joshua tree in the yard.

How diverse things are between my Pacific Northwest home and this open desert! Mirror opposites, my Cascadia is so green. The fragrant scent of the ocean and pungent evergreen trees. Even the grey clouds that frequently bring rainy days always give way to the cherished sun. The sacred waters nourish all we see. So very different in the desert and I experience a twinge of homesickness.

Here the sun and the sacred waters are cherished too. Just in a different way. Here water is life more than anything. The sun illuminates, radiates. The sky is immense and endless. Everything is clear and unshrouded. I can see. It feels as if everyone can see all the aspects of me too. I am very visible. I cannot hide. I cannot pretend.

It does feel a little bit strange and uncertain. A bit alien, unprotected. I need time to get to know this land, to delve down deep and feel a part of the framework, essence and rhythm of the realm. I need to be patient, to wait out the tendency towards feeling misplaced. I will soon feel at home.

In a new space I do best when I completely immerse myself. I need to get to know it intimately; to spend the time required to make a comfortable home and understand the pieces of the whole, explore the parts of the puzzle that make the desert, and embrace it totally.

I treasure this new scene, a moonscape of alien terrain. The winter can be crisp with clear blue sky and occasional chilly winds that fly down the mountains white on the horizon. The air is dry, sucks the moisture from me and doesn't give it back. It is full of static and my hair is all frizzy. Every time I reach out to pet her, Luna jumps with a staticky shock. Old dry riverbeds hold no hint of water. Occasional flash floods wash out sand in a blast of sudden winter storming, so quick, not much chance to soak it in and then it's over.

I can't deny the twisted beauty of this desert, but I also cannot stop wondering just why the hell anyone decided to live here in the first place. Why did the homesteaders settle here, living in tiny "jackrabbit" huts, the desert rats, amid the scarce water sources and extreme temperatures? These days there is air conditioning and basic access to some water, which is what makes it habitable for the people who presently live here. Modern conveniences have changed life. Times are getting dryer, however, and access to potable water is getting more difficult. I imagine there may be a time in the future where humans will no longer be able to live here in the numbers that they presently do.

Well, I begin the task of settling in, always a spiritual journey. I take in and begin to internalize the beauty. The once strange twisted trees, pink-gold-tinged bare soil, and spikey plants are becoming familiar to me now. I don't know if I can ever get enough of these magnificent Joshua trees. I continually marvel at their artistry, the wisdom I somehow seem to derive from them, the tranquility they impart. Will they ever be just ordinary to me?

I find my quiet spots, warm spots in the desert, melt into the sand and open my head up to the blue sky. There is a stillness within a little nook I have found amid the boulders, nestled in the sand. Wrapped in the distant winter sun's pale warmth, not the blistering furnace of summer, it is mild and mellow. I feel tucked in and happy.

Late winter is the time of year that things are kind of slow in Joshua Tree. It is the respite before the tourists arrive. Not many "lookie-loos," it is mainly locals coming out to play. The cacti have not yet bloomed. The Giant Tortoises are still buried in the sand. It's too cold for most people to backpack or camp in the desert. Some restaurants thin out their menus, serving only the tried-and-true dishes appreciated by the locals; basic dishes and drinks without catchy names. Entertainment and music are almost nonexistent during the lull. Many small businesses and tourist traps close down for a little vacation. By March things will be in full swing again, until the extreme heat arrives in June.

A block or two up from the cross-state Highway 62 there are no traffic jams, no roar of the unending vehicles racing across the scene. Just streets of sand, roads that stretch miles across the flats and up into the hills. Endless sight. Endless quiet. Endless peace. I am away from the pavement, away from the crowds. I can breathe deeply, breathe in clean air tasting so very delicious. The calmness just seeps, creeps into every pore, every crevice. Every muscle relaxes, unknots, melts throughout.

The desert is a ballet in still life. It is as if the trees are dancing behind your back, and then when you turn your head to look, they freeze in graceful pose. Twists and twirls are caught in stop action mid-stride. The backdrop of stark rock places and faces is just so, as if to highlight, to emphasize, the peaceful scene below. Then a breeze comes up and the dancers sway and rock, rooted in place.

A study in contrasts, in stretches of endless serenity, blue, blue sky spreads forever. Bare golden sand and twisting stems of the juniper form a blanket under the sun. The surreal rock sculptures are formed by summer heat searing, winter freezing and cracking. Land opens to rolling dips, crevices where little things live hunkered, seeking scant shade, warmth and moisture. Further along the yucca begin, bigger now, and the twisted, tufted olive-green Joshua tree tipped by yellow spires.

The open stretches of sand reflect brightly here. No shade from light any way you look at it. Stark, open, calm, right, it reflects ancient times, before humankind, before all knowledge. Dreamless past unravels, unwinds. Sands reflect my own face.

Perched atop the boulders, nestled in a cove of rock and sand, I view the day unfold. The town spreads out below like spilled water on the desert floor, soaking it in. On the horizon rocks are piled perfectly atop each other, lopsided, haphazard peaks of gold. Plucked by some prehistoric hand, they are balanced but looking as if casually tossed aside. Boulders cascade like a still life waterfall.

Out across the vast expanse, the desert stretches miles. Joshua tree and yucca dot the scene, melding into white sand closer to the hills, so far away that distance is meaningless. Hard, clean, windswept. Little puffs and then a dirty haze rises. Sands shift in gusts of air.

I smile contentedly. Like i could stretch out, unencumbered, and sleep for a thousand years. Like the Joshua tree, I feel rooted in the sand as if I could grow cheerfully towards the sun indefinitely. I am a piece of the whole; elemental, important. I have a purpose in the scheme of things, although I may not know exactly what that purpose might be.

When I stop and think about it, I am still truly amazed that I am here. So many daydreams in the past few years about venturing out on my own have dissipated like smoke. Thoughts about where to go, a million choices; I could have gone abroad to explore other countries, ancient homes of my ancestors. Perhaps I could have immersed myself in the foods and wines of Italy, the ruins of ancient Greece, all the cultures of old. I could be exploring my ancestry, my history, right now instead of being here in the desert. I could have traveled with a group of elders through Europe or Asia, along the Silk Road, ridden the Orient Express, hiked in the Alps, explored the Great Wall, or wandered amid the ancient ruins of Thrace or the Druids. All so fascinating, full of stories and wonder.

I have been led here, and there must be a reason.

Terry M. Mandeville

desert as a ballet

curtain rises, sparse clouds part
sky clear above a work of art

still of morning has passed, quiet has given way
ushering in the ballet

hushed whispers mount, play their parts in winter as music
begins alternating speed and volume, gusty desert winds

crooked limbs of the joshua tree all day have given me shade
now they sway a bit, one arm beginning in an easy slow wave

sparse desert grasses with a gust move in a frenzied quiver
undulate then shiver

a pair of quail zig zag onto the scene, darting without hesitation
they dance across the sand, top notches bobbing in syncopation

road runner dashes out stage left, another dancer in his beak
twisting turning squirming
exits stage right with staccato shriek

under my legs runs a startled kangaroo rat
she squeaks her part ...and that is that

CHAPTER 3

WINTER IN THE DESERT

winds, storms, cold

Terry M. Mandeville

winter in the desert

winter was never so bright, ignited
never so many stars at night
endless sight, light, delight, just right

stark proud joshua trees reach one by one
toward distant sun
cherishing the season just begun
anticipating rain to run but there has been none
shunned, done

greens of yucca pointing, leaning
are they dreaming of climates teaming
with moisture and rains gleaming?
sheen unseen, in-between

bright sun radiates
through my body percolates
through my veins and around my brain it circulates
wait, create, gestate

it gusts and blusters
it huffs and puffs strength as it musters
down from the hills thrusting
from the snow's luster
it clusters, flutters

Journal Of An Old Hippie Chick In The Desert

wind whistles and rumbles
across my ears it tumbles
and all i hear is jumble, mumble, fumble

blows the dust, the sand
in waved bands
across parched land expands, slams

howl and scour windblown sand of such power
keeps up this pace until the wee hours
devours, towers, showers

whips my hair into my eyes
strands that refuse to be contained or tied
smack side to side
as i try to hide, cry, sigh

the gusts ebb and flow
and so it goes
blows, overflows

continuing at will
clouds racing along the distant hills
continuing until
the night brings the still, fulfill, refill

Winter in the Mojave is fickle. On any one day it can be sunny and warm. I bathe in the warmth, sitting outside on the daybed in my shirtsleeves soaking it all in. The next day a cold wind blows down from the mountains and I have to bundle in my knit cap and down parka or stay indoors. The air is mostly dry, but sudden rain squalls can descend at any time and pelt huge raindrops upon my head. The backdrop of mountains is capped with snow, and snow falls sometimes on the hills surrounding me. Occasionally it can even snow down on the flat of the desert where I am.

Today the wet windy tendrils, like those of the Pacific Northwest, have found me; the Atmospheric River rages. It blows, clatters, pounds and pours; it keeps it up. All night it thumps and bumps. Now Luna must go out to pee. She is trying to wait out the rain, hating to get wet. Finally, she cannot wait any longer. Darting out and returning quickly, she comes in soaked, bedraggled, and unhappy. The yard floods, standing water has no place to go and cannot soak very far into the baked sand. The washes are full and chisel out channels over the road. I don't think I should be going anyplace soon.

After a while the rain stops, although it is apt to start up again at any time. I have cabin fever and am longing to get out for a bit. It would be an adventure, right? I splash along in the truck, circumventing the deep standing water, bouncing up and down over the newly carved crevasses, and feeling the truck tilt big-time where the water has washed away parts of the road.

Merging onto the paved highway everyone is going their normal high speeds downhill towards the low desert. As the road hits the flats of Morongo Valley, we hit the pooled water by the stoplight and hydroplane through. No one else even slows down.

A rainbow fades in over the hills, suggesting a pot of gold someplace back in Yucca. I pull off the highway to gawk, a bit along a sand road that quickly becomes a rutted pathway. The rainbow becomes more vivid as a shaft of sunlight shines in from the north. Painted neon purples, reds, greens, oranges duplicate and form a double rainbow. A work of art. A spectacular masterpiece. I sit for a bit taking it all in.

Another morning, I emerge from my cocoon to warm still sunlight streaming in the window, beckoning. Can't fool me. I know this winter desert sun for what it is. It attempts to dupe me with brightness. January is just not exceedingly warm in the desert, even when the sun is out. During the day I might shiver. Temperatures at night drop even further and the dog water freezes solid. February will come, though, with its own unpredictable climate. One day my fingers freeze, the next Luna is laying stretched out, panting, on the sand in the sun.

I take a chance and journey into a secluded area of the desert. Walking for a time, I seek a suitable place to sit and write. An easy-going, mild warmth envelope me like an ocean wave, caresses me. Scent of desert carries an offering to my senses. Sage, creosote, agave, musk, mineral aromas permeate. Deep endless golden sands stretch to the horizon, blending to blue sky which is also endless. Sun warms a bit with each minor climb in the sky, warms my face, my shoulders. It warms the sand under my feet even in the thin winter light. The white of the cliffs fluctuate to pinks and russets, depending on the angle of the sun.

Then a cool breeze wafts through, clean, refreshing. Arms of Joshua tree and fronds of palm dance subtly in a slow romantic hula. It's clear and beautiful still, yet I am beginning to wonder if I might be taking too much of a chance to sit here for long. It is still winter after all. I am wondering if this gentle wind might be a forewarning of more. Luna loves the scents on the wind, but the blowing sand makes her sneeze. Then the breeze fades and again all is still.

Dried blossoms of last summer stick to bushes like dust on a whiskbroom. Remnants of last year's bloom still cling to crowns of the Joshua trees like tiny bare twigs. Life hides in winter. Tortoises bury under mounds of sand. Rattlers nestle between slabs of rock. Squirrels burrow in their holes. Birds fly farther south. Yucca bushes bear only their solid sharp spines. Joshua trees abide and hope for water.

Suddenly the wind kicks up again. A frigid blast shoots down from the snow-capped mountains, reminding me again that winter continues. It whips the sand into my eyes, my ears, my hair; sand that somehow adds grit between my teeth. It whisks into nooks and crannies. Gusts push the pine needles under my chair, huddling and piling there like a nest. Things sway, but at least there are no huge hemlocks or firs to fall on me. My hat sails away and I run to catch it.

Clouds roll in. The sky darkens. Rain begins, a misty drop or two becomes more and we are getting wet. Rain in the desert. I imagine the trees and brush eagerly lapping it up through the straws of their shallow roots. Rain in the desert. Somehow redundant to escape from the downpour back home to experience it here, without the lush emerald of the underbrush, without the dark green of the forests. Rain in the desert. No coyote calls. Animals huddle together to stay dry and warm. Luna cowers with uncertain primal fears of thunder.

We look for shelter in this flat part of the desert. Rain splats against big boulders, holding no caves here. Stands of Yucca and squat scrub have no roof to deflect the deluge. Wind pierces my rain-soaked clothes. We look for shelter and all I can see is a clump of bushes up against a boulder, larger as we approach. Dusty olive green and grey, I think them just a block in the path to skirt around. The branches are tightly woven, intact, with no way in. We circle around to gain another perspective. Still nothing unusual, like a footnote, quietly forgotten. We circle further and there seems to be some sort of an entry next to the rock that opens into a fairy-like shelter from the storm.

After a quick scan for critters, Luna and I crawl into this little desert cave made of bushes. It is fairly dry, cozy and warm, decorated with branch hangings of nature; abstract haphazard weavings, scented with pungent sage. We stretch out on a bed of dry grasses upon warm sand. Rain patters on the roof, wind rattles. There are small gaps to look out on the world and to let in the sun when it finally returns.

We emerge to a washed clean tableau as the sun materializes again. Watered by winter rain, the Joshua trees raise their bushy green heads to the sky. They seem happy now. Healthy. Vigorous. Majestic in their twisted glory. Readying for the late winter flowering. Aching for the heat and long days of summer solstice.

A bird peeps as if to test out the weather. Then a little puff of wind appears, a whisper of a breeze, as if to say the storm is over now. It caresses my ear and moves on its way. I hear it skitter gently into the distance, to the hills, sliding like a small wave. Then all is still again.

I make it back to my little home in the desert as the sun goes down and the night temperature rapidly drops below freezing. Stars delight in the early setting of the sun and shine their hearts out before the clouds roll back in.

In the morning snow falls, a few flakes at first, becoming flurries, and then starting to stick. It lines pockets in the rocks, sticking to the lee side of the Joshua tree trunks. Undisturbed cold white stretches across the desert floor with much more settling high on the hills.

The golden hills of the park are white now, whitewash painted over the granite. Layer upon layer of vanilla ice cream, speckled with chocolate chip rock outcroppings. This is a winter backdrop that lies below the ice and snow of the San Bernadino mountains.

Little quail tracks dot the yard, squiggly paths in circles and curlicues. They have been looking for food under the snow. Layers of roadrunner prints run across, toes facing front and back, so I don't even know what direction they were travelling. Canine footprints outside my gate are proof that the coyote have been here, silently, only a few minutes before. Soundless stealth in the still of the snow.

The snow ceases to fall. Cold sun quietly climbs higher, trying its best to warm. Snow is melting quickly for now. These are short winter days with little time to accomplish the task. The sun goes down all too soon, temperature plunging again, and the snow melt freezes. The sky clouds and snow falls again. Then by the next morning it is as if there had never been any such a thing as snow. The air is crisp, the land dry once again.

The unpredictable pendulum of winter in the desert.

Terry M. Mandeville

pantoum for winter in the desert

it is cold today in the desert
winter has truly come
frozen sand and dirt
hold together as one

winter has truly come
weak sunlight glows in the sky
hold together as one
for warmth, you and i

weak sunlight glows in the sky
snow falls on the distant hills
for warmth, you and i
we stoked the fire until

snow falls on the distant hills
i remember when
we stoked the fire until
we were warm again

i remember when
with relief and mirth
we were warm again
it is cold today in the desert

CHAPTER 4

WRITING IN THE DESERT

words flow

Terry M. Mandeville

desert haikus

i came here to write
winter desert is my muse
stalled by distraction

procrastination
delays creativity
requires slight nudge

warm inspiration
lies beneath the desert floor
ready to burst forth

writing comes easy
words rise up out of the sand
if i just pay heed

softly scratching pen
across the yellow paper
creates word pictures

Journal Of An Old Hippie Chick In The Desert

I came to spend a little time in the desert for many reasons; to get away from the endless stretch of dreary rainy days, to start a new adventure, to find myself once again. Another primary goal has been to open new avenues for my writing. I long to find focus in a setting where the words flow and inspiration will flood around me.

Two writing projects are in progress, and indeed I have made headway on them here so far. Unrelated prose and poetry come at me from all directions, though, and I find that I also must record these words and images that come as a separate task.

The first step of my creative process is to write in my journals by hand. A worn and weathered bag with different colored pens and markers is always kept handy. The bag also contains several spiral notebooks. I haul the bag with me into the yard of my abode, or bring it with me in the truck when I venture out. I try to classify the notebooks by project; however, they frequently get blurred, merge, and provide jumping off points for one another. I write freestyle, initially without structure, without adhering to tradition or style. Words blend into phrases and sentences, and then into prose. Thoughts become poetry, songs in my head that rhyme and alliterate unbidden. I draw clumsy little scribbly drawings in my journal that serve to illustrate my words, and help me find a way to describe and explain.

I move outside to write, sometimes in the park, other times in the yard, even stopping while on a walk. Some days, as it is wintertime, the icy winds sweep down from the mountains and I sit bundled in my winter parka and hood, with a blanket over my lap. I feel the momentum to write. The notions are there and the words are flowing. I eagerly get out pen and notebook and begin to jot it all down. As the cold wears on, I begin to feel chilly and my ability to write becomes impaired. I find, finally, that I must move inside when my fingers get too frozen to hold the pen and Luna begins to shiver and whine.

Other times the warmish breeze floats, wafts desert scents my direction, and caresses me. I feel lazy and unchallenged. I am easily lulled into peaceful slumber or distracted into daydreams. I try to focus, to fight the pull of procrastination. Generally, at those times it is of no use and I give in to the luxury of relaxation.

What do I write about? I seem to yearn to paint flowing word pictures of desert life right now. Thoughts and sensation flow through my pen onto paper. The Joshua trees speak to me and tell me their stories. The sands whisper ancient words to record. The sun melts into me, energizing the coursing impressions and bringing them to light.

Other days the desert lends clarity to the stories I am already in the middle of writing down. Back home I am scattered, distracted. I have a dozen stories started and going nowhere. Here in the desert words and rhymes seem to drift about and I can reach out and pick them like cactus blossoms. I can see the flow of the story and move with it toward the end. I am writing a story about my mother but I have been getting too bogged down with past hurts and anger. Here I can untangle those knots and write her story more clearly. I am also writing a story about Luna from her point of view. Here I can see the light that she is, what makes her happy, and how her dog mind works.

I hold on to so many things; dragons, my mother's books, Bob's shot glasses and old stories, my dad's old bathrobe, refrigerator magnets, old poems. I wear the same favorite clothes for decades. It is so hard for me to let anything go. I hoard ideas, photographs, old camp songs. Perhaps if I am able to put their stories into words I will be able to finally let them go.

The emotions are the hardest to set free. I have bottled up that old anger and disappointment that I still hold toward my mother; the chasm of mutual misunderstanding that was our relationship. I have bottled up that resentment over the loss of time; decades spent over-nurturing; tending the needs of so many others while neglecting my own. I have bottled up the sadness over ancient unrequited loves. When I can write about these things, when I can set it down on paper, I can truly bottle it all up for good. I can stick a heavy rock in it and hurl it into the river.

Rarely am I able to initiate the process of writing on command. Rather it usually comes unbidden, at odd times. In the bathtub a set of descriptive phrases come to me and I recite the fountain of words to myself, vowing to remember. By the time I emerge I have become distracted and I forget. In the middle of the night, when I wake to pee, I have a thread of enlightened thought but I cannot find a pen and paper in the dark and it is lost by morning. While doing a chore my mind will wander and a story sometimes makes an appearance. I have the best intentions to write it down as soon as I can. I don't. While listening to music outside on a moonless night my thoughts wander along a line worthy of expanding. I am too comfy and relaxed to stop and document it. Many times, while I am driving in the truck a flash comes and I call my answer machine to record the gist of it. It's usually not enough to get the entirety of it back when I get home.

Back in my abode I move to the second step of my writing process. With access to electricity, and the ability to read my laptop screen without the shine of the reflecting sun, I transcribe my work into my ongoing files. I refine and rework the words. And further refine and rework.

Yes, out in the desert I have found my muse.

In ideal moments I get on a writing jag and the words pour forth. The setting is right, the impetus is there, the distractions are kept at a distance. Luna is self-occupied and happy. I am warm and all is comfortable and conducive. Honest thoughts stream to the forefront and the goal is to expel the clutter so that what is left is the essence, the kernel of what is to be written down. I can get rid of the excess, stripping bare to the root. Naked real and true. Catharsis, and what remains is mine to record. These are times, rare back home, when the breeze clears out my head and I am acutely aware. Nothing to jumble the senses. Clear thought. Focus, observation, concentration. Not incumbered by shame or stupidity. No doubts, no regrets, no guilt about what I should write. Just the bare bones of what is, what was, what will be. These are times when I can let it out, let it go. The words spew forth and spread across the paper in an extremely satisfying way.

On occasion in the desert, it seems as if the mundane seems to expand. Everyday things suddenly shift, seen in a new light. These are inspiring times for new writings. Things before me become novel and wonderous as I try to share the sensation, to describe, to explain. To find just the right words.

There are so many spots throughout the desert and around my abode that awaken my senses. Yes, there is insight and the words do flow. I have said that distractions are minimal but to tell the truth there are a few. I try to reach a balance.

One of my favorite places to journal is in the park, even though it is prone to touristy crowds at times. Since I usually take Luna, and dogs are not allowed on park trails, it isn't feasible to go very far on foot. Besides, I like to sit in my comfy folding chair when I write.

Parking lots and main roads in the park are usually busy places, and not too inspiring for focusing. Despite this, I have found a couple of dirt roads with all kinds of ominous signage that seems to discourage the majority of the tourists from venturing very far into their depths.

Geology Tour Road winds through the rocks and Joshua trees, eventually ending down in the low desert and Highway 10. After a certain point a 4-wheel drive with high clearance is required in order to rumble all the way down to the end. The road tilts as it traverses mounds of granite rock and rough ruts, and some portions are particularly steep. It is a washboard of a sand road; dusty, and rock-strewn. Some tourists start down this road. Most turn around at the first chance.

This all conspires to lead me to drive a bit down the road, find the perfect spot to pull over, haul out my chair and some water, amble a short distance, put Luna on the long tie out, sit down and write. It is still and noiseless. There is the occasional jeep, the people inside looking at me curiously as if I am some crazy desert rat perched out here on the sand. They move on and I don't give them a thought as the desert vibes just seem to seep up in through my feet and into my brain.

Even though it is just a turn out off the road, the area is alive with desert vegetation, rock towers, golden sand, roadrunners, ravens, and far horizons. Luna sticks her nose in all of the little varmint holes in the sand and around the creosote bushes. She hasn't gotten bitten by anything yet.

So, I sit and write here. Here by a lonely turnoff on the side of a rutted sand road in the middle of Joshua Tree National Park. And I feel as if I am smack-dab in the middle of the universe. I form a deep understanding of just how very small I am. I proceed to try and project thoughts from that grounded perspective. Emotions and epiphanies are difficult to put into words. I can feel it but I often find it difficult to explain myself. Here, incredibly, the words just seem to come.

Terry M. Mandeville

playing with words

words becoming poetry
as they shuffle around
i play, adjust
for impact and sound

a game i am so fond of playing
with paper and pen
combining thoughts
rearranging bits over again

the cadence of a phrase
the rhythm of the line
the exact meaning of a set of words
the way they combine

CHAPTER 5

DESERT AS A CANVAS

the desert is art

Terry M. Mandeville

desert as a canvas

a palate of rocks and soil
muted hues of mustard and anise
flecked with crystal lights and speckled pearl

the sun is a ball of bright white light
radiating rays of cream and eggnog
bright baby blue endless sky streaked
with cloudy wisps of ivory mists

adobe painted hills and slopes shaded in distance
existence in layers of pewter iron smoke

bare branches fuse to become hues of plum
magenta of bud bumps on creosote trees
feeding fuzzy yellow bumblebees

dusty greens of cacti and pine, ochre, marigold
the younger branches entwine in jade
nubs of grassy tufts, fresh tea stained
strain to push through earth
after long awaited scant rain

joshua trees stand in shaggy straw-dyed trunks
tapered with tufts of seaweed green
a few crowned with tassels of tangerine

perforated skeletons of cholla twigs litter brown ground
mere stone tinted shells share space
with finished indian rice grass the shade of old lace
bare willow a study
in muddy charcoal and steel at the trunk
merging to burgundy hints
bark with stretch marks that glint mustard
topped with small orbs of custard

thorny ocotillo branches in pigeon-grey
snake up from the desert floor
more like stationary sea plants
waving away toward the sun

mesquite limbs crookedly dance
perchance in time to the wind
dangling leaves spin like silent windchimes
of lime and tuscany-yellow sunset

clouds screaked with gold
then the sky, the earth everything that glows
bathed in rose
sun sets
washing from the canvas all hues
all the golds and blues
night brings only shades of black and gloom
under a sliver of a silver moon

Terry M. Mandeville

This Mojave Desert is, well, it is just plain and simply ...art. All by itself it is such a stunning, incomparable, soulful work of creativity. The sky of deep blues, colors of the sunrise, sunset and moon rise are the palate of the universe.

The swath of the milky way twinkles in the inky night. Puffy clouds form horses, dragons and elephants. Arrow straight crisscross of jet trails sometimes appear as ancient runes before they expand and dissipate.

Serpentine Joshua trees in spiky greens and golds please the eye. Lacy teddy bear cholla skeletons beckon to be gathered and crafted into wall hangings or earrings, or just a bouquet of branches in a vase. Tortured and twisted limbs of old mesquite form abstract art. Pointed yucca create exquisite Japanese fans growing from the sand.

The texture and multicolored rock archways and faces are masterpieces of style. A perfect 10-foot-tall Heart Rock that nature carved has been just plunked, upright in the desert, and it captivates lovers. The curves of Arch Rock produce graceful elements of fine architecture. Nature's human-like sculpture that is Skull Rock is mask-like, worthy of a Mardi Gras parade, or a Kukeri performance. Patterns, shapes, symbolism, art, and beauty abound in the rocks.

The desert also inspires humans to unique artistic creations of all kinds, and arouses artistic appreciation in even the casual tourist. I am inspired, and I write.

From time to time, I attempt to make some visual art too. I have never felt adequate in painting or drawing. The picture in my head is never what gets onto the paper. I sit at the outdoor table, white paper before me, water in the cup, paint pan open. A used paper cup holds a variety of paintbrushes. I choose a wide brush, dip it in the water and then twirl it in the red watercolor square. A swath watery pink streaks across the paper. How can I put the image there? Can I build it? I add other colors, I make it darker. What is it? I try to add detail, define, shape. It remains a messy blob, not even one with character. A flop. Garbage fodder.

More white paper before me. I dig out my assortment of pens, pencils and markers from deep within my old tattered bag. Can I draw what I see? I scratch, I scribble. Dots and lines. Round and fill in the curves. Nothing matches the scene. Nothing makes sense to my eyes. Just a bunch of uninspired scribbles and I toss the paper in the recycle bin. I want so much to depict the image in my mind; to make the white paper into a semblance of art that touches my spirit, my soul. I will keep trying, and Joshua Tree is certainly the right atmosphere, if there ever was such a one for me.

The village of Joshua Tree truly is art heaven, a tugging distraction from my writing, and it is all fascinating. The bordering towns contribute their art vibes too. As if the surrounding beauty is not enough, every day I discover new human-made sculptures in hidden places. Works of Christian and Hindu inspiration and flowing abstracts carved from rock lay hidden in the hills. Welded metal works dot the roadsides and people's yards. Wood carvings, petroglyph inspired art, mystical drawings, paintings of spectacular scenery are scattered about, as if in a scavenger hunt, waiting to be found. The sides of buildings exhibit murals of animals, plants, people and history. Neon brightly painted houses stand out on the desert sand. Stunning, unique and awe-inspired architecture dots the landscape with reflections, stonework, and contours.

In the village there are several sculptures. Out and about I find the parking lot next to the Saturday Farmer's Market. As I exit the truck, I find a plaque that says this is "Turtle Island." An island? Where is the water? I guess it is a traffic island between the highway and the Farmer's Market area. The plaque notes that the "island" is dedicated to Al Mackin, known as "Mr. Turtle." On the "island" stands "Murtle the Turtle." At about four feet tall and ten feet long, she is the world's largest reproduction of a tortoise. The real tortoises are presently in hibernation until it gets warmer, so this sculpture is probably the closest I will get to the real thing. From the 1950s to the 1960s Joshua Tree used to hold an annual Turtle Day with Tortoise Races and an accompanying parade. Murtle began her life during that time as a float on wheels made from a wire and wood frame covered with plaster and cement. Since the turtles that raced were actually desert tortoises, now declared an endangered species, the races were discontinued and Murtle was covered with concrete and donated to the Joshua Tree Chamber of Commerce.

Also on "Turtle Island" is a carved brown stone sculpture entitled "Spirit Climb," created by Yucca Valley sculptor David Falossi. From a distance it just looks like a marker, a monolith. As I get closer, I see it consists of the back side of a rock climber, with long hair flowing free, climbing an eight-foot rock. Mr. Falossi has said that the sculpture symbolizes "what we all have to go through in our own spiritual climb" and relates to the many rock climbers that regularly come to the park.

In Joshua Tree one person's trash is another's art form. Assemblage Art is everywhere. Old broken-down furniture is repurposed. Junk is recycled into entirely different configurations. Salvaged castoffs are reassembled and rearranged. You can tell where the artists live by observing the installations surrounding their houses.

Up the hill from the village, near where I am living, is perhaps the most unique, unbelievably strange and wonderful art museum ever, the Noah Purifoy Outdoor Desert Art

Museum of Assemblage Sculpture. I can walk there with Luna and see something new each time I go. Mr. Purifoy collected junk; old toilets, sheet metal, guitars, Commodore 64 computers, boots and shoes, bailing wire and rebar, fences, toys, record players, kitchen utensils, typewriters, bicycles and gears, farm machines, ragged clothing and shoes, vacuum cleaners, old tire and, oh, so much more. He gave these worn out rejects a brand-new life, putting them together in a new form. He made them into over 100 works of art. I can imagine him looking at an old television set with faraway eyes, envisioning the new representation that he could create there.

Locals left Noah their "garbage" and he made art; welded things together into creations from his mind. A carousel of old computers sits behind brightly painted panels. A water fountain labeled "white" stands next to a toilet labeled "black." Old lunch trays are put together into a rollercoaster. "Adrian's Little Theater" made from leftover palates beckons me to get up on the aging stage platform and recite some poetry. Shopping karts and ladders form a train atop a track of old shelving rails. There is even a dragon welded together from an

Terry M. Mandeville

old plow and metal parts. An outhouse has feet sticking out from under it. There is an archway of toilets, bicycles balancing atop an old shack, a graveyard with crosses made from old wood pieces, fences made of old tires, and a kart of old folding chairs. His mind went in devious directions, and left artistic chaos in its wake. Visitors wander about the ten-acre museum; some in aimless direction, some in awe, some in confusion, some with scorn, but always there is a reaction.

Nearby, the more than 400 Simi Dabah Sculptures cover eight acres. Mr. Dabah has welded scrap metal into sculptured creations. There are art pieces of all sizes, some more than 20 feet tall. The sculptures exist at various levels. Some are set on the earth, others buried below the ground, and still others seem to float in the air. The metal rusts in cubes, concentric diamonds, hoops, funnels, wheels, starbursts and suns. There is no public entrance and the exhibit is all surrounded by a fence; nonetheless, it can easily be seen from the sand road that surrounds the expanse of art.

Journal Of An Old Hippie Chick In The Desert

The towns of Joshua Tree (JT), Yucca Valley (Yucca) and Twentynine Palms (29) are meccas for many quirky museums and shops. Countless little stores, art galleries and museums exhibit a variety of paintings, sculptures, native art, crafts, and other art work. It takes dedication and determination to get a business going and maintain it amid the extreme temperatures and the wax and wane of the tourists. Some of the businesses, especially the smaller stores, seem to come and go. Others are able to stay the course over years.

The Art Queen strip just east of the saloon is a hub of eclectic talent. The World-Famous Crochet Museum is an old re-purposed "One Hour Fotomat Booth." It hides in a courtyard tucked behind a line of little stores. A wide assortment of colorful crocheted items of all kinds are crammed into the shelves, all squished next to each other. Creatures such as frilly poodles, laughing kangaroos, white bunnies, climbing monkeys, smiling dogs, teddy bears, monsters, mermaids, dolls, and cartoon characters sit so close to one another that it is difficult to differentiate. Other crocheted items include a decorated Christmas tree, rugs, pillows, pot holders, various emoticons, and some food items like tacos and mushrooms and fruits. Faded crocheted blankets hang over the surrounding fence. Items are sent in from all over the world. A crocheted crocodile named "Bunny" has her own Talk Show at the Beatnik Café.

I pop into the Art Queen Gallery, next door to the Crochet Museum, to see Sheri Elf, a friendly folk artist, singer-songwriter, and seamstress. She displays and sells her paintings, stickers, patches, and re-purposed art made from fabric and wood. Political T-shirts and recycled clothing hang from racks. Several other stores in the Art Queen strip accent the area with sculptures, stained glass, and decorative pots.

Next, I visit Jeff at his Beauty Bubble Museum of Hair and Beauty. It is not only a museum; it is also a functioning salon! Jeff has collected over 3000 pieces of hair and beauty memorabilia and he has it all stashed in various little rooms about the salon. The antique electric permanent wave machine looks like a torture device. Jeff is most proud of his masterpiece wig mannequin head sculptures, the "Hairsterical

Gals," named "the perm," "the pompadour," "the beehive," "the flip" and "the afro." The wig-heads consist of old plastic and metal beauty waste: perm rods, rollers, barrettes, combs, clips, brushes, ponytail holders, head bands, and banana clips which are fashioned into crazy hairdos.

Many of the high-end short-term rental houses are littered with art pieces. Some are artistic and architectural wonders in themselves, although I could never afford the cost of the rent to stay in those. Mojave Moon Ranch, a 220-acre private property known as the "Jewel of Joshua," houses the world-renowned South African artist Daniel Popper's work, "Transmission." Made of concrete, steel, and glass mosaics, it rises some thirty feet above the desert. The face of a goddess towers over all, adorned with colorful glass mosaic creations. She is guarded by two sets of open-palm hands on both sides.

Private yards and acreage outside of town offer their own little artistic touches, many times in the middle of nowhere. Cast iron sculptures. Old mining equipment found in the desert, reconfigured and painted bright colors. A mountain of colorful bird houses. Mosaic tiles. Various stone and wood signs. An old satellite dish made into a native inspired painting. Hanging crystals. Dinosaur statues. A long line of black mailboxes, all the same, way out far from any road. A phone booth made into a doorway. A hand-built clay kiln. Line of bicycles doing wheelies half buried in the sand. Blown glass fashioned into a tree.

In the town next door, Yucca, there is Desert Christ Park, a sculpture garden by the late Antone Martin. He created 35 statues based on the New Testament of the Bible. He felt that these figures would be responsible for saving the world by discouraging an atomic war. Let's hope it works.

The Glass Outhouse Art Gallery is just east of 29, the town on the other side of JT. The artwork includes recycled art, such as a bicycle fence, a VW bug morphed into a turtle, and a gym full of skeletons. Elaborate metal art includes a winged dragon, a rooster, and a colorful peacock. There is a giant Pepsi can, pirate ship, metal grasshopper, a little bug café, and a church. Next to the church is a small graveyard where "all bad things are buried such as war, greed, malice, and hate." And there actually is a glass outhouse on the property, a functioning outhouse made of one-way mirrors.

Inside Joshua National Park there is, of course, the natural beauty that is art in itself. Hidden away are also native painted and etched pictographs and petroglyphs, some created more than 1000 years ago. The bleaching sun and scouring wind-blown sands have erased countless of these ancient works of art. Many of those that still can be seen have all but faded. A few can only be found now in areas that are protected from the elements in hollow boulders and caves.

I am intrigued by this indigenous art, and long to search out the meaning behind the symbols. On the whole, they seem more primitive than other petroglyphs in the Pacific Northwest, maybe more symbolic. Many of the symbols are obviously of the sun, which stands to reason as the sun always dominates the scene. Sun is the giver of life, necessary for the growth of food. There are spirals which symbolize migration. Spiders symbolize creativity and the weaving of fate. Diamond shapes may represent rattlesnakes, guides during vision quests. Small bisected circles could be direction markers, denoting direction of a nearby spring or oasis. There are also symbols that look like rakes, crosses, wheels, fish, water, and people. Some colors are still visible and these hold meaning too. The colors were made with ochre, berries, and various vegetables. It is ancient art and strikes a chord within, perhaps in ancestral memory, although admittedly my DNA does not show any Native American in me.

Rhythm of Life Earthworks are essentially art in symbols. They are up in the hills above Yucca, atop a long steep hike to get close. The geoglyphs were created using over 460 tons of stones, stacked to create the immense designs. It is part of a larger project that is meant to form a chain of 51 gigantic stone sculptures around the world, a vision for connectivity by Australian sculptor Andrew Rogers. Rhythm of Life is a collaborative endeavor, designed and constructed by the local community as "an optimistic symbol of life and regeneration." It is meant to be an "echo" of the pictographs left by the indigenous peoples in the area.

artwork of the gods

smooth faced pinks and gold
a history of old, old tales
artwork of the gods
perhaps placed for our brief nod in time
stark beauty rising out of the desert sod

molded
folded
artistic rhythms to behold
leaning boldly
as if placed just so by another
an artist, creator
the mother

patterns and shades
caves smoothed by time
reflect light
now fleshy pink like playdough
like feet and toes
sticking straight up
from the sandbox

Terry M. Mandeville

ancient rock villanelle

these rock monoliths gleam
jutting out of the land
scoured and clean

frozen molten tubes lean
rise in odd angles to stand
these rock monoliths gleam

baked by heat, cracked by freeze
carved by some sentient hand
scoured and clean

there is a pattern to the scene
mother earth's plan
these rock monoliths gleam

rough stucco finish seems
eaten and polished by sand
scoured and clean

maybe some alien force beamed
and just set them down out of hand
scoured and clean
these rock monoliths gleam

CHAPTER 6

STORIES OF THE DESERT

in the beginning

Terry M. Mandeville

stories of the sand

sands spread across the desert floor
sparkle in the ebbing sunlight
born of ancient rock
worn by winds and waters' might

if only the sands could talk
these tiny crystals of gold
so much history
so many tales of old

oh, the stories that these sands
must have withstood
witnessed
understood

ancient tales that have been protected
carried by the human creatures
they tell of life's beginnings
in the parables of the teachers

I can feel ancient spirits all around me, old as the earth itself. It is an easy place to feel at one with the earth. To feel a descendant of Mother Earth and Father Sky, as we all are.

The first humans in the area, tens of thousands of years ago, were nomadic Paleo-Natives. They moved from place to place in the cool and wet Mojave area south of the glaciers. As the area became drier, they moved elsewhere and the Pinto culture arrived. These people also were a very mobile nomadic people with seasonal camps. They did not leave many permanent artifacts in their wake, although they wandered the area from 5000 to 2000 B.C.E.

New native tribes arrived. These were the people who made the petroglyphs depicting a rich ritual life. According to the Maara'yam (Serrano) creation stories, the village of Mara at the oasis in the present 29 Palms was occupied from the time the Maara'yam arrived on earth until the mid-1800s. The Nüwü (Chemehuevi) occupied the oasis after their war with the Aha Macave (Mojave). The southern part of the park was Kawiya (Cahuilla) territory. Other native tribes that lived in or frequented the Mojave Desert included the Vanyume (Beñemé), Tataviam, Kitanemuk, Kawaiisu, Tübatulabal, Southern Paiute, Navajo (Dine), Hopi, and Shoshone.

Although much of the original teachings and histories of the native peoples has been lost through extermination and assimilation of the native way of life, some oral history remains. The native tales of wisdom, resilience, and the very beginnings of life have a place in my heart.

The native stories tell of alien planets, animal people and the wisdom and skills of the desert dwellers. They open up another perspective. There are some similarities between tribes, and with many other cultures and religions. In the beginning there was nothing on earth, no life, only darkness. The people were created, or came here, by some powerful primal forces.

I like the stories of beginnings on other planets. Does this explain the petroglyphs with flying humans, aliens at Giant Rock, or the directions to build the Integratron? Is this evidence of an advanced civilization from another world immigrating here? Over the millennia, did the struggle to survive wipe out that memory? Now there is a great plot for a novel!

Terry M. Mandeville

Aha Macave (Mojave) Creation Story

Sky and Earth met far in the west and had children. A son, Matevilye, was the first born. After him came the younger brother Mastamho, all the people, the animals and the plants. Matevilye created the people and led them to the east, arriving at Ahavulypo, which was the center of the earth. He gave the people their names and their commandments. Here Matevilye died. Fly rubbed her thigh and created fire to light the first funeral pyre for him. Mastamho then made wind, hail and rain to wash away the remains of the body.

Mastamho went north and shoved his stick into the ground, making water spill out. Stomping the ground with his foot four times he caused the water to flow southward and form the Colorado River, which he gave to the people. The people shouted four times and made daylight, the sun, and the moon. Mastamho taught the people how to plant seeds in the fertile floodplain of the untamed river. These are the age-old customs of the Aha cave.

He gave the people bird-singing and dancing. He created the medicine-men, and separated the six tribes. Then he sent off five of the tribes to different countries. The sixth tribe, the Mojave, he ordered to stay in the desert. He taught the people to use the indigenous hallucinogenic east root of the plant Datura, the "Old Woman," in religious sacrament. In the visions resulting from the Datura, lost items were found, enemies and evil magic were revealed.

Terry M. Mandeville

Nüwü (Chemehuevi) Creation Legend

It is important to note that Nüwü myths may not be told during the summer. If this taboo is violated, someone will be bitten by a rattlesnake.

There are two time-periods of the world. The dawn era was when animals were people, having both animal and human traits. They could change shape or disappear as they wished. At the close of this era some of these creatures went north, others were changed into the animals that we see today.

In the beginning there was only the Immortal Water. One day down from the sky fell Hutsipamamau'u (Ocean Woman) in the form of a worm. She created Sinawava (Coyote). She created Tivaci (Wolf) as his wise older brother because Sinawava had no common sense. She also created Tukumumuuntsij (Mountain Lion). These were the "Primeval Four," the four great predators. They floated in a basket in the ocean.

To form land, Hutsipamamau'u mixed a piece of the sail and some of her skin into the sea. She faced west and laid down on the land she had made, spreading out the earth with her arms and legs. When Hutsipamamau'u was satisfied with her task she sent Tivaci north and south to inspect the new land. He found it fit. Sinawava went east and west and also found it fit. There was room for the people.

Terry M. Mandeville

The Broken People of the Nüwü (Chemehuevi)

Before time began, there was Pokoh (Old Man), who was made of the soil. It was he who created the world. Pokoh had many blankets in which he carried around gifts for men. He created every tribe out of the soil where they used to live.

One day Sinawava (Coyote) found a basket near a spring of the Colorado River. It had something inside and so he opened the basket. Quail jumped out and scattered and the first Kawaiisu (Animal People) were set free.

Old Woman lived on an island in the sea. Sinawava came upon the daughter of Old Woman, Poo'wavi, while hunting. He immediately desired her, and Poo'wavi became pregnant. She tried to drown Sinawava as she ferried to the island to her mother. Sinawava turned himself into a water spider, running across the water to reach the island before Poo'wavi did.

Sinawava found Old Woman sitting by her brush house weaving another large storage basket. She put Poo'wavi's fertilized eggs into the basket and gave it to Sinawava with strict instructions to take it directly to his older brother,

Tivaci (Wolf), who was wise and would know what to do with the contents. Sinawava set off to do as instructed but soon the basket started jiggling and moving. Of course, Sinawava, being Sinawava, became curious. He took the basket to the desert and opened it. Out swarmed the people of all the tribes. They ran in all four directions to populate the earth. When things had calmed down Sinawava looked inside the basket to find only the broken remains of the people who had been crushed in the exodus. He brought the basket to his wiser brother for help. Tivaci was able to heal the broken people and make them strong. He taught them to find water and sustenance in the desert.

Sinawava returned the healed people to the desert and told them that this land was now theirs. These people were now smarter and stronger than the others. They would find richness in the land that others reviled. From that day on the Chemehuevi have lived and died in the place where they were created.

Terry M. Mandeville

The Many Worlds of the Tubatulabal

The Tubatulabal of the Sierra Nevada valley did not have a supreme deity. They did believe that at one time the plant Jimsonweed was a man. He made himself into a plant so that the people could use his roots as medicine. Jimsonweed was the link to help from the mystical world.

They believed that their world was populated by various mystical beings, human and animal spirits, who lived in nearby rocks and streams. The spirits had to be treated with respect, otherwise these beings would bring hardship and destruction. They believed that the plants and animals could hear all that was said by the people. These beings had made the soil, mountains, oceans and other elements of the earth.

They believed that there were many worlds throughout the universe. Some of the worlds have come to an end, and some have yet to exist. In some worlds the people crawl. In others they may fly, swim, slither or walk on all fours. In this world we just happen to walk upright on two legs.

The creation story of the Tubatulabal tells of Coyote who remade the earth following the world flood. He also found fire, started the division of labor, and brought death. He is a trickster who lied and conned the people.

The creation of Kern Canyon occurred when Hawk and Duck, who enjoyed racing each other, repeatedly raced back and forth, bouncing side to side. They carved out the canyon as they raced up the Kern River.

Terry M. Mandeville

Navajo (Dine) Creation Story

In the beginning there were four corners, with four cloud columns that contained the elements. Black Night was to the north, Blue Daylight to the south, Yellow Twilight to the west, and White Dawn to the east.

The First World of the Navajo of Southwestern America, Nihodilhil, was dark and foggy. It was a small island floating in a sea of mist. On this island was only one pine tree, insects, spider and black ants, and the bee and wasp people. These beings were "Mist People" without form. Great-Coyote-Who-Was-Formed-in-the-Water came in the form of a human male. He was hatched from an egg and knew all that was under the water and all that was in the skies. And this small world was crowded. The people fought and were unhappy. They later became the humans and fauna of the world.

The Second World, Nihodootlizh, was blue. First Man was created here where the Black Cloud and the White Cloud met. With First Man came a perfect ear of white corn. Where the Blue Cloud and Yellow Cloud met, First Woman was formed, and with her the yellow corn.

The Third World, Nihaltsoh, was the Yellow World. This was where the other living creatures were formed. One day Water Buffalo became severely annoyed when First Woman urged Coyote to steal his children. Water Buffalo created a huge flood and First Man and First Woman were driven out of the Third World.

The Fourth World, Nihalgai, was the Glittering or White World. It is our present world.

Terry M. Mandeville

Nüwü (Chemehuevi) Tale

of How Tavutsi Cooled Off the World

Tavapëtsi is the name of the sun, and Myarago-Pitsi the moon. The moon would only emerge from his den in the dark as an animal accompanied by many dark crows.

In the beginning the world was very hot. It was too hot to live. One day Tavutsi (Cottontail) hit Tavapëtsi in the head with a large rock. This broke off huge pieces of the sun and lessened the heat. This was the way Tavutsi made the earth habitable.

Another tale about the Lone Woman is illustrated in several petroglyphs in the Mojave Desert. Tavapëtsi impregnated a mortal woman by projecting rays of sunlight into her at sunset and she gave birth to twin sons. These petroglyphs are symbolic of the Spring Equinox, the beginning of the growing season and the fertility that spring brings to nature.

Maara'yam (Serrano) Story

About How the People Came to This World

In the beginning Pakrokitat created humans and three goddesses. His twin, Kukitat, disapproved of the humans and wanted them killed. The humans divided into groups and fought with each other. Many attempts were made on Kukitat's life. Finally, the attempts succeeded when Frog poisoned him, and Coyote stole his heart. Kukitat was cremated on the shores of Baldwin Lake in the San Bernardino Mountains. In the fighting, all the Mariña Serrano were killed except one man, from whom all present Mariña Serranos are descended.

The Mamaytam Serrano (or Yuhaviatam, which means "people of the pines") lived in Southern California. They originally lived on a different planet that was somewhat similar to this one. There were too many people on the old planet, they just did not fit anymore. Finally, their leader brought the people to Maara', a very beautiful place. The different tribes of the Yuhaviatam scattered, only the Mamaytam, Muhatna'yam, and Maareng'yam were left at Maara'.

The Serrano believe that all plants, animals, and rocks are sentient beings. They were created from humans who wanted to be transformed into other beings. In the beginning the lord was living in the Mojave Desert with all the people. He asked who wanted to become deer. The lord transformed those who volunteered. The deer danced the deer dance. They sang about their creation story and what they did. They still behaved as human beings. Some were sad, they missed their homes but they had to go into the hills to live. It took time to learn to walk on their hooves. Eventually they did.

Now, when a human hunts a deer for food, the kill is brought to the ceremonial house. The body is sung to and prayed over all night.

Ivilyuqaletem (Cahuilla) Creation Myth

According to the Ivilyuqaletem of Southern California, for a very long time there was only darkness and the Two Nights in the world.

Once, during a storm, there was a flash of lightning. From that lightning two strong twin boys were born of the Two Nights. They were named Mo-Cot and Mo-Cot-Tem-Ma-Ya-Wit, which means "creator." The brothers were the first people of the world. They lived in the air as there was no earth and no water. Darkness surrounded them as there still was no light.

The brothers said, "We must create now." Mo-Cot created tobacco and he called it Man. Mo-Cot-Tem-Ma-Ya-Wit created a pipe and he called it Woman. Then they created fire so they could smoke the tobacco.

When the brothers tried to come down from the air to stand, they could not because there was no land to stand upon. They made rock and set it in place. It was not steady enough to stand on. They tried to make snakes to hold the rock. The snakes were not strong enough. They tried to pile more rocks around. It still was not enough. Finally, the brothers made some big spiders. The spiders wove webs around the rock to hold it and it worked. They made more of the earth out of rock and used the spider webs to hold that together too.

The earth grew fast. It was not still. Mo-Cot and Mo-Cot-Tem-Ma-Ya-Wit made wind to even the earth out. The earth still would not calm down. They made red and black ants to go out and steady the earth. That did not work either. At last, they tried turning up the edges of the earth and filling the bowls that formed with water. This finally succeeded in steadying the earth.

Mo-Cot and Mo-Cot-Tem-Ma-Ya-Wit created Ow-Il (dog) when they smoked the tobacco. However, the tobacco smoke hurt dog's eyes and that is why dogs cannot see well during the day. They created Is-Eel (coyote) and Is-Eel helped to create the rest of the animals.

Mo-Cot-Tem-Ma-Ya-Wit and Mo-Cot wanted to make people like themselves. They took the moist earth and mixed it with white, black, yellow and red clay. Of this they made the people but they could not see what the people looked like. They blew some stars into the sky but that was not bright enough. Together they blew the sun into the sky and it moved rapidly. They could not catch it as it sank into the horizon. From then on, the sun came up above the horizon every morning and went down at night.

The brothers argued about death. Mo-Cot-Tem-Ma-Ya-Wit wanted no death but Mo-Cot said, "If there is no death the earth will soon be filled up with too many people."

The brothers fought. Mo-Cot-Tem-Ma-Ya-Wit was so angry that he tried to destroy everything. There was darkness and fire, earthquakes split the earth. Where Mo-Cot tried to hold the land together, mountains rose. Finally, Mo-Cot-Tem-Ma-Ya-Wit gave up. These brothers had argued, and this is how it came to be that all brothers have argued ever since.

Now the people noticed that they were different colors. The white clay had made white people, the black clay had made black people, the yellow clay had made yellow people, and the red clay had made red people. The white people were not happy about being without color. They tried to be dark by rubbing different clay on their skin, but it came right off. They were so angry that they went away.

The rest of the people also wanted to leave. So it is that most children go away and start their own lives instead of staying forever with their parents. "As things were done in the first beginning, so they have been done ever since."

Mo-Cot stopped the red people from leaving and kept them with him. These are the people of the desert.

In the desert you can hear the Two Nights sing to their children every night, a soothing humming song. The people are lulled to sleep, and sleep until the sun rises in the morning.

This song continues to sooth all the earth's children to sleep.

CHAPTER 7

JOSHUA TREES

twisted guardians of the desert

Terry M. Mandeville

the joshua tree

twisted tufted
green and brown limbs uplifted
prickly spikes point and scrabble
crowns as a convoluted pineapple

unrestrained
pushing up through rough terrain
shape in the night as a man in flight

raised arms loop in celebration
as a woman greeting the sun
head bent taking in earth spirit
rooted in place

graceful crazy snake shape
a work of art, each unique

soldiers that never speak
standing in silent rows and packs
not once marching to attack

they thrive
uniquely painting the barren landscape alive
standing their ground
they surround the soundless scene

I could write about the Joshua tree endlessly. It is ancient, fascinating, symbolic, beautiful and grotesque; and the stuff of legends.

In 1844 the American explorer John C. Fremont said of the Joshua tree; "Their stiff and ungraceful form makes them to the traveler the most repulsive tree in the vegetable kingdom."

Joseph Smeaton Chase wrote; "It is a weird menacing object... One can scarcely find a term of ugliness that is not apt for this plant."

As I drive between Yucca and JT, spread out forests of Joshua trees twist to the hills on either side of me. I do not find them repulsive. Quite the opposite. They make me smile.

When I enter the park from the northwestern side there are hundreds of thousands of Joshua trees, in places spread like spaced out forests of wavy limbs to the rock cliffs. Most of the Joshua trees in the world are here. They roll over white and gold desert sand, framing the outcropping of rock and climbing up hills. Stretching to dots on the horizon. They are misshapen figures like some alien garden. Ancient twisted life with arms that rise toward the sun, turning and bending stiffly away from the wind, grown gnarly and twisted. Their shredded grey-brown trunks with reedy bark jet upward; branches leaning and pushing towards brightly tufted pointy pompoms.

Twisted shapes. Convoluted snake arms. Crowns of tufted spikes. Shaggy trunks, shredded bark. Abstract. Asymmetrical. Resilient. Majestic. Powerful. Magical. Inspirational. Spiritual. Glorious. Supernatural. Unique. Exquisite. Each a still life painting framing different movements in a dance. Every time I see these amazing specimens, I am awe-struck by these art forms right from the mind of Dr. Seuss. I always loved Dr. Suess.

Strictly speaking they are not trees at all. Once classified as a Lily, the Joshua tree is now designated as a yucca member of the Agave family. It just resembles a tree. These Joshua trees are the largest yucca in the world. Scientifically they are called Yucca brevifolia (not to be confused with the Mojave yucca, Yucca schidigera, which has bigger leaves outlined with curling threads). The Spanish named these unique trees "izote de desierto," meaning desert dagger. Native peoples have many names for this magnificent plant; it is called "soap tree" by many Native Americans, the local Cahuilla call it "hunuvat chiy'a," Western Shoshone referred to it as "umpu," the Serrano call it "choor-martsh." The Southern Paiute refer to tree as "sovarampi," believing them animated by magical beings of the same name.

Different stories suggest how these towering yuccas got the name Joshua tree. It seems that the name was given by Mormon settlers who were guided by the Joshua tree as they crossed the Mojave Desert in the 1800s. One version maintains that the shape of the tree reminded one of the bible stories in which Joshua kept his arms lifted to the sky in prayer to lead the Israelites to Canaan. Another account says that the trees were named for their pointed leaves, shaped like blades, a symbol of Joshua's army. Still another story suggests that the bushy leaves may have reminded the Mormon band of Joshua's beard.

Terry M. Mandeville

Joshua trees are useful; they are vital in many ways, providing food for both humans and animals. Fruit and flower buds can be baked, boiled, or crushed and used in making cheese from goat's milk. The roots can be added to soup, or sliced and pan-fried like French-fries. They have been listed as an ingredient in Shasta Root Beer, key to the beverage's foamy head when poured into a glass. Seeds are eaten raw, roasted, ground into flour to make little cakes, or dried and stored for the winter. The leaves can even be boiled and eaten.

Natives of the Mojave and Western Sonora Desert have appreciated the life-giving properties of the Joshua tree since prehistoric times. Leaf extract of the Joshua tree is used for cosmetics and is found in several commercial shampoos and skin care products. Soap has long been made by pulverizing the roots to wash clothes, bodies, hair, and in native rituals of spiritual cleansing.

Traditionally local native peoples have created tools and weapons from the tree. Leaves are soaked in water, pounded with stones to separate the fibers and made into sandals, belts, rope ladders, fishing nets, hoops, prayer sticks, chant arrows, rope, and cord. Baskets are woven from root sheaths and leaf fibers. Yucca juice was mixed with charred pine or juniper that had been struck by lightning to make a poison applied to arrow tips. Paint and dyes are made from the leaf juice and the Joshua tree has been fashioned into innumerable works of art over the ages.

There are many traditional medicines and folk remedies made from the extract of the Joshua tree. The saponin steroids found in the leaves, trunk and roots are said to have many healing properties. They reportedly contain chemicals that might reduce swelling, act as an anti-inflammatory for arthritis, alleviate gastrointestinal discomfort, and have antibacterial and antifungal properties. People have used Joshua tree products for osteoarthritis, high blood pressure, joint pain, migraine headache, diabetes, and many other conditions. A tincture made from the roots is used to manage pain during childbirth.

The skeletons of the Joshua tree are light and decompose quickly, not dense enough to be used in constructing durable structures. They were used by white settlers as fencing material, and they sometimes burned the wood. As a fuel it does not provide much long-lasting heat.

The trees are home to many birds, lizards, insects, and the Yucca Moths. In fact, the moths' breeding ground of choice is the Joshua tree. They lay their eggs in the creamy blossoms and go on to pollinate others. The big, juicy seeds are the favorite food for their caterpillar offspring. The trees do not produce nectar, so the moths are their only pollinators.

A stationary dance scattered across the landscape; randomly reaching out, snaking up. These are gothic creatures; otherworldly, alien. Still life hula dancers, topped with straw hats. Crowns of green spears.

The Joshua tree is an ancient and powerful spiritual guide for many indigenous peoples. Native Americans believe it to bring rain and good luck. These trees have been sacred throughout history as examples of how to live, grow, transition, change and die with patience. Cultures around the world view trees as sacred symbols. The Joshua tree is said to be "a place to find peace," that it has a neutralizing and uplifting field of energy. Many people, including myself it seems, are drawn to these beings to soak in the healing atmosphere!

They are symbols of survival and perseverance in the middle of a merciless and unforgiving environment, demonstrating how beauty and life can still blossom in challenging times. Every one of these beings has withstood the most demanding environment on earth and yet they persist. They are remarkably adaptive and determined. Born in the desert, they thrive with little water. They survive scorching heat, sandstorms, arid conditions, frigid cold, and winds that are blistering in the summer and bitter cold in the winter. In spiritual practices, the Joshua trees are widely revered for their powers, often as a symbol of love, hope, faith, protection and guidance in ceremonies or rituals. The leaves, flowers, and fruits are given up to the heavens offering blessings through prayer and meditation.

The multi-armed symbolism of the Joshua tree is not lost on me. Related images come from many directions. I see unending correlations, outstretched hands reaching for meaning and guidance. I see the multi-armed Trimurti Hindu gods; Vishnu and others have many arms that represent preservation, protection, strength, motherhood, power, change, time, creation, knowledge, new beginnings, wisdom, and luck. They embody the "Cosmic Dance" and the "removal of obstacles" and they give direction.

In a way it seems as if the Joshua trees are sculptured works of art illustrating the religions and legends through the ages. The many armed and headed Buddhist Bodhisattva, the Judeo-Christian God as "a dwelling place underneath everlasting arms;" Allah's "outstretched hands." Many ancient mythologies can be interpreted in the Joshua tree.

Much is written about what has been learned by others from these living beings. Resilience, patience, individuality, detachment, maturity. How to find your true self. To slow down and take your time. To let go of attachments that are not supportive. To find balance in all things. To be patient with yourself. To pay attention to the phases of the moon and how this affects energy and emotion. To learn that recognition of talents may show up only with learning and maturity. To let go of the expectation of others. To learn the amount of nurturing needed in order to thrive. In rough times it can lead to growth and understanding.

There are other things I see in the Joshua tree from nature. The Milky Way shines down at night with far reaching tentacles. The many long arms of the octopus are said to symbolize life's complexity, intelligence, and immortality. In mythology the five arms of the starfish represent thoughts put into deed; each arm symbolizing new direction, outlook, and pathways toward growth and understanding.

Joshua trees have been around for 2.5 million years. Originally native to Mexico, Central and South America, the ancient Shasta Giant Ground Sloths ate the plant's large seeds and excreted them as they traveled. This animal seems like he was made just for a diet of Joshua trees. His large height enabled him to reach the top of the trees as his big tail stabilized him. He had eight-inch claws that could bend the branches down to his mouth, swallowing the fruit whole and making it unnecessary to chew and crush the seeds. The sloth wandered around the southwest and enabled the plant to migrate quickly during the Pleistocene era.

I cannot help but try to get to know this magical being, to entangle myself in her arms, to absorb the ancient knowledge. Old Woman Joshua tree, I wonder just how many years you have been here? What have you seen? Do the years go by quickly? Do you have ancestral memory that recalls the sloths that 32,000 years ago scattered your seeds throughout the world? Did dinosaurs tramp the sands around you? Did you see dragons in your youth?

Up through the sands, you have survived droughts and winter winds, making your way between human devastation. The first peoples respected you, tended you, listened to your wisdom. You gave clothing and food in return. Then the careless ones swarmed the land, took the land. Excesses, waste, pollution, carelessness. They burned, cleared, terraformed in their own image. They didn't see your beauty. They called you twisted, evil, Satan's spawn. Mistreated for hundreds of years, they dug you up and chopped you down for "progress."

In the early 1900s the Bureau of Land Management removed trees for oil and gas development. Smog from Los Angeles comes through San Gorgonio Pass, bringing ozone, soot, and nitrogen which fertilizes invasive grasses. These grasses fuel wildfires. In 2020 a fire killed more than a million Joshua trees in the Mojave National Preserve. Many times the visitors to the park disregard regulations, camping on delicate land. Vandals cut down Joshua trees and carve roads through the area.

There are fewer young Joshua trees growing from seed in today's world. The fruits that bear the seeds require cool, wet springs, which are getting less and less frequent in the Mojave. The fruit also hangs on tightly to the tree, sometimes for more than a year. The seeds are held in chambers surrounded by the fruit which, after a month or so, turns fibrous and makes it difficult for the seeds to escape.

Baby Joshua trees can also "clone," that is they sprout from roots and branches. This allows them to recover quicker after a flood or fire, but conversely it prohibits them from migrating to more hospitable territory. By 2100, some studies say only 0.02% of the habitat in the national park will remain viable for the Joshua tree. It has been said they are "a symbol of our utter failure as a society to address climate change."

Old trees bent with age drop, sad broken limbs dangle. Amputated they leave empty stumps that droop, forlorn, with forgotten past glory. In death they turn darkened charcoal. These fallen soldiers lie like empty tubes on the surface of the desert. New green growth attempts to rise from mummified remains. How many years will they continue alive?

The Joshua tree now primarily grows in the Mojave Desert of California, Nevada, Utah, and Arizona. A few can be seen in the Sonoran Desert among the Saguaro cactus of western Arizona or alongside the pines of the San Bernardino

Mountains. They are very picky about where they can thrive; they only survive between the elevations of 2,000 and 6,000 feet. I drive through the park, down towards Cottonwood Oasis, and I see the Joshua trees becoming smaller, and then amazingly they disappear completely as I get to the Colorado desert.

Now, the possibility of migration to more habitable areas is slim. Without the Giant Sloths to help, the only natural vehicle are the ground squirrels. Some humans are banking the seeds and researching more hospitable land. It is now illegal to kill or damage a Joshua tree, and there is legislation to include them in the endangered species group. Will that impact their demise? I cannot imagine this land devoid of these spectacular works of art.

Here, in my yard on the hill above town, there is just one lone Joshua tree. It isn't very old by Mojave Desert standards. It only has 2 branches, not very tall, scrawny and thin. It may not be long for this world. How did it get here all by itself? Were there once others?

Joshua trees grow slowly, two or three inches a year. It can take them 50 or 60 years to reach full height. They live, on average, about 500 years. Some are much older. A single tap root can tunnel 30 feet down to find water. Another shallow root system spreads out, like a spiderweb, from the plant to collect any rainwater that falls from the sky. They grow from 5 to 40 feet tall with a diameter of 1 to 3 feet. If they have had rain, a winter freeze, then warmth at the proper times, they bloom. When and where depends on the elevation and varies year to year, site to site. They may begin blooming in February in the lower elevations of Pinto Basin, Yucca and JT. At higher elevations they might bloom in March or April, or even May or June.

I am lucky, I get to experience the bloom. White-green rosettes develop on long stalks at the tips of some branches, amid shiny green spikes. The bud grows, and opens up slowly into a creamy white, waxy bunch of curled petals covered by a thin green coat. Looking kind of like a gigantic mound of popcorn in a green bowl, the bloom is spectacular in this late winter sunshine. The otherworldly aura of the Joshua tree makes the whole thing seem like "pods" out of "Invasion of the Body Snatchers." Surely such a glorious tree in bloom, such a magnificent flower, must have a delicious odor? Unfortunately, no. Smells kind of like cleaning fluid.

These prophets amid the desert, structured as if to commune with the gods. Surreal, mystical, magical, wistful. Harbingers of peace, tranquility, stability. Beings of beauty, they stand in solitude quietly worshiping the earth.

So, I settle in for writing time under a glorious tree in bloom, insects buzz all around the blossoms. Moths flutter inside the flower and collect pollen. Birds flock around the flowers and an old Scott's oriole nest hangs in the branches. A lizard searches around the base for some tasty insects, and Luna is right after it.

Joshua Tree / Yucca Fries Recipe

Ingredients:

3 cups oil (high smoke point)   2 lb. Yucca/Joshua tree root

1 Tbsp. fine sea salt   1 tsp. black pepper

1 tsp. cayenne   1 lime, zested

1 tsp. paprika

Directions: Joshua trees are protected and may not be harvested; other yucca roots may be substituted. Soak roots overnight. Heat oil to 350 degrees in Dutch oven. Mix spices. Peel roots, cut into strips, add to oil. Fry to golden brown.

Season with spice mixture and lime zest.

Hispanic Cream of Joshua Tree / Yucca Soup Recipe

Ingredients:

2 Tbsp. olive oil

½ onion, chopped

2 Tbsp. minced garlic

¼ c. recaito
   (Hispanic bell pepper base)

5 c. chicken bouillon

¼ tsp onion powder

¼ tsp dried oregano

paprika to taste

pepper to taste

¼ tsp sugar

fresh cilantro

24 oz. yucca root

Directions: Soak roots overnight, chop. Heat oil over medium-high heat. Add onions and garlic, cook 10 mins. Add recaito, cook until bubbling. Add yucca and bullion, bring to boil, reduce heat, simmer covered, 25 mins. Blend soup in batches and pass through fine mesh strainer. Extract as much liquid as possible. Simmer, stir in remaining seasonings and sugar. Top with cilantro.

Joshua Tree / Yucca Shampoo and Soap

To make an aromatic shampoo that leaves hair very shiny, find a small to medium sized plant that can be dug up without too much difficulty — even a young bush will yield enough roots for a dozen or so shampoos. Remove all loose dirt and chop with a hatchet into manageable pieces. Cut off the hairlike extensions and the outer root covering. Chop into smaller chunks and pulverize into pulp until color has changed from white to light amber. Shampoo is ready to be used, dried, or frozen.

Clothes can be washed by adding shredded yucca root directly into the water. The shredded or sliced root can also just be left out by the sink for hand washing like a bar of soap.

Jicarilla Apache Origin of Yucca, Sheep and Cattle

Naiyenesgani was looking for monsters. He killed all he found. He climbed to the top of the mountain and looked in all directions, but failed to find any more monsters. Frustrated, he threw his staff out into the desert and said to the Mojave tribe: "You will make your living through this." The staff landed on the sand and became a yucca. This is why the Mojave tribes live upon the fruits and leaves of the yucca plants. Naiyenesgani poured some water and washed his hands from the blood and poison of all the monsters he had killed. He threw the bloody water in different directions. He told the Mexican tribe, "With this you will live." The material that he washed from his hands became cattle and sheep. This is why the Mexican tribe has many sheep and cattle.

Terry M. Mandeville

How the Joshua Tree Was Created

Yee Naagloshii lived alone in the desert. A few times during the year the buffalo hunters would come, following the buffalos to find food. When the hunt went well, they would celebrate with a great fire and dancing. Yee Naagloshii did not know how to dance, but she wanted to learn. When she told the buffalo hunters this, they laughed that she could not dance. They made fun of her. She became angry and killed some of the hunters. Others of the hunters she froze into Joshua trees so that she would not be alone anymore. She also wanted the people to know that they should not make fun of her. This was how the Joshua trees were created and why some of them look like dancers.

CHAPTER 8

SISTER AND BROTHER COYOTE

the tricksters

Terry M. Mandeville

brother coyote

brother coyote
open land and sky
to the tune of your song
solitary howl
then it isn't long
until the others join with staccato harmony

brother coyote
calling us out
with your throaty melody
into the silvery night
singing joyously

brother coyote
soft fur pelt of winter
bright eyes
sly
ever the trickster
calling us out to play
and stay with you
for the night

Old Trickster Coyote has come to visit. I see him leading his pack up and down the trail by the house, past the rise. They go by in the morning to hunt, and come back in the afternoon to their dens for a rest. The whole pack looks sleek and well fed on cottontail, ground squirrel and jackrabbit.

The leader, bold and beautiful in his fur and confidence, has come back by himself this afternoon. He stands at the edge of the patio peering into the house at us for a long time. For once Luna is still, mesmerized, and they lock eyes. Something passes between them and he leaves. Shaking off her hypnotized state at last, Luna of course goes into a confused ballistic state of outrage. Barking, shaking and running in circles, her ridge hair standing straight up, she cannot be consoled nor calmed for quite a while.

After dark the trickster returns. His long melodic howl draws in the others of the pack and they surround the house, beckoning Luna with their yips, trying to make us believe that their numbers are greater than they actually are. "Come on out, dog! Come play! Come join us for dinner."

Luna looks confused and huddles with me on the bed. I think she knows what they mean by the invitation to dinner and she silently declines the offer. The pack continues their serenade for fifteen minutes or so. When no morsel of food emerges from the house, they wander off.

Coyotes usually yip to tell the others in their group where dinner is. It is meant to frighten, and it did. Do they regularly make this attempt to lure unsuspecting dogs out to be their dinner? Or are they just welcoming us to the neighborhood? I doubt it. Are they upset that we are in their territory, their land, their home? We are the intruders, the trespassers, the aliens here.

The pack has never come that close again, although I see them every day on the trail at twilight and early in the morning, just passing through. I hear them each night up in the hills. It's like we have passed some kind of a test.

Little Sister Coyote regularly slinks gingerly on the opposite side of the fence along the trails she treads so often. She moves with stealth, low to the ground. Her sunken eyes dart right and left, alert for pray or predators. Her pelt is scraggly in uneven shades of black and grey, with bare patches perhaps of mange. She is ever so skinny, with stick legs, and looks very cold. Her tail is long, straight, sturdy; neither lifted in play nor lowered in fear.

A loner, without a pack, without a mate; perhaps older, aged, sick, but dangerous still. The rabbit or roadrunner are a possible dinner. Maybe a cat or a small dog. Coyotes have even been said to steal babies. I think perhaps that is just an old parable meant to keep children from wandering.

She smells the scent in the air. Caution. Life stirs nearby. Foe or friend ...or food? Sister coyote slows her movement, warily becomes the sand around her. Silent, still, she searches the breeze as it ruffles her fur. Assessing, gauging danger versus food, she inches her way closer. Curious, hungry, serious; her eyes burning coals. She spots the creature. She stands waiting, watching, debating. Her prey is quicker. Opportunity eludes her and she turns. Hungry for another day. She quietly retreats, her eyes still burning.

The coyotes are at home here. They roam their territory, as they have since antiquity. They are protective and possessive of the land of their ancestors, their history, their own. The coyotes tread their path, as they have for untold years. They know the canyons and the hills. They know who belongs here and who does not. Stealth, sly wisdom, ancient knowledge.

The scientific name for the coyote, Canis latrans, is Latin and means "barking dog." The name coyote is based on the Aztec word "cóyotl" which means "trickster." Coyote is Sinawava to the Chemehuevi, Ma'ii to the Navajo. Coyote is referred to by the names desert dog, song dog, yodel dog, pasture puppy, canine cockroach, prairie wolf, sage wolf, brush wolf, fawn killer, cased wolf, little wolf, American jackal, hooter dog, walking buzzard, yelp dog, and a long line of other rude names.

Sinawava is Joshua Tree's Spirit Animal who shows up when needed. A contradictory character, Native Americans consider the Coyote a creator, an Ancestor Being, and a trickster. In the ancient stories, as a Creator, Coyote shook a blanket in each cardinal direction and created the land and water. As an Ancestor Being he is a spirit who is often contacted in dreams or trances. Simawava's energy can be both disruptive as well as beneficial. He is a shadowy figure that can be humorous or frightening; a balance of playfulness, vanity, wisdom, foolishness, cunning, power, simplicity, greed, laughter, adaptation, clarity, creativity, contradiction, and reluctant heroism. He comes to humanity when life is being taken too seriously. He teaches us to heal and cope by laughing at our mistakes.

Coyoteway is a special healing ritual for the Coyote Clan in which Coyote plays an important part as the totem sponsor. When offended, it is felt that the Coyote People (coyotes, foxes and wolves) respond by causing illness. The goal of Coyoteway is to restore harmony with the Coyote People. Over several days Coyote is honored in ritual, singing and prayer. The singer mediates between Coyote and the person that needs to be healed.

Terry M. Mandeville

Coyote is a frequent character in many of the area's native creation tales and traditional stories. According to Chemehuevi beliefs, Hutsipamamau'u took some dirt, mixed it with her sweat, and created Sinawava. Sinawava is cunning. He has no common sense so Hutsipamamau'u made Tivaci (Wolf) and Tu-kumumuuntsij (Mountain Lion) as brothers for Coyote to temper him with their wisdom.

He is a trickster in Chemehuevi tales; irresponsible, disobedient, full of humor, and continually causing trouble. In every battle he is the first to be killed, and the last to be revived. He also is a helper to the people, teaching wise lessons on dealing with stress, calming the spirit, and adaptation. He taught the people how to make arrows and use tools.

He may be the universal trickster but he is also a hero and teacher in countless Native American mythologies. He is responsible for many things, including the Milky Way and the diversity of mankind. Coyote is helpful to humans at times, at other times his impulsive acts create trouble for everyone. Sometimes he dies because of his own carelessness. He is always resurrected. Coyote can shape shift with ease, sometimes he takes a human or other animal form.

There are "more stories about Coyote than stars in the sky." In one tale Coyote angers Porcupine as he tricks him out of a portion of buffalo meat. There is another story in which Coyote is tricked into dumping his grandmother's acorns into a river. Another tale tells of his transformation into a platter in order to be heaped with food to satisfy his voracious appetite.

Coyote and the Giant

Giant ate people, especially small children. One day Coyote said to Giant, "If you allow me to break your leg, I will spit on it. It will then be healed and you will be able to run as quickly as I."

However, this was a trick. After healing, Giant found that he was much slower and could not outrun anything, even small children.

Terry M. Mandeville

Sinawava and the Constellations

One time the fire god, Black God, made some stars and carried them out into the desert in his blanket. He began painstakingly placing them into the night sky, one by one. He arranged them into patterns, the constellations, so that travelers could find their way.

Sinawava became impatient. He grabbed the blanket and tossed the rest of the stars all at once into the sky, forming the Milky Way.

This is why some stars are dimmer than others, because Black God had not had time to light some of them on fire before Coyote blew them into the sky.

The Navajo believe the Milky Way provides a pathway for the spirits traveling between heaven and earth, each little star being one footprint.

Sinawava Finds the First Horse

Grandson was sent to visit Sinawava and told not to enter the cave lying between their houses. As it began to rain, he decided to spend the night in the cave anyway. When he awakened, he discovered that he was covered with hair.

As he left the cave, he was followed by the mountain sheep to his grandfather's house. Sinawava saw the sheep and noticed that one was much bigger than the others. Sinawava thought the big sheep would make a great meal, but Tivaci revealed the true identity of the large sheep and urged Sinawava not to kill Grandson, but to feed him some bunchgrass instead. Sinawava agreed and decided to settle for killing some of the smaller mountain sheep. Grandson went off to spend the night with the other mountain sheep.

The next morning the two Sky-Down-Feather Brothers were hunting. Eldest Brother recognized the big sheep as a boy and warned Younger Brother. Younger Brother killed the sheep anyway. The slain body suddenly turned into a boy wearing moccasins. The two brothers then butchered the body and flew away.

Sinawava found blood and hair of Grandson, packed it in a basket, and plotted revenge with Tivaci. They hid some water, but saved out some next to the firepit. Parotsok

Itapitsi (Black Spider) then wove a web in the sky's hole. Sky-Down-Feather-Brothers were thirsty. They could not find water until Younger Brother spotted the water that had been saved out. Older Brother suspected that Sinawava was hiding there. The brothers tried to trick Sinawava by taunting him. Each time, Sinawava almost revealed himself thinking he had been discovered. Each time Parotsok Itapitsi yelled a warning. The brothers dared to drink and Sinawava threw a hot stone from the fire. The brothers tried to fly away and were trapped in the web. Then, Parotsok Itapitsi climbed down the web, biting and killing the brothers. Sinawava returned to where he had left his grandson's remains and found that his grandson had become a horse.

Skunk Outwits Coyote

Coyote was walking through the desert one day feeling very hungry when he spied Skunk. "You look hungry," Coyote said. "Help me trick Prairie Dog and we will get something to eat."

Coyote told Skunk to lay down on the road, puff himself up, and play dead. Then Coyote went to Prairie Dog's burrow to invite him and his neighbors to dance over the dead body of Skunk, their mutual enemy.

"Let us stand in a big circle and dance around the body with our eyes closed," he said. "If anyone opens their eyes, something bad will happen."

As soon as the foolish prairie dogs closed their eyes Coyote leapt forward and killed one of them. When the dance was finished and everyone opened their eyes, they were surprised to see one of their group lying dead on the ground. "Oh dear!" said Coyote. "Look what happened. He must have opened his eyes and that caused his death!"

Coyote urged the prairie dogs to dance again over the dead. In this way, Coyote continued to kill them one by one.

Meanwhile Skunk built a fire and began roasting the kill.

Finally, suspicious, one prairie dog opened his eyes. "Coyote is killing us!" he shouted, and all the prairie dogs ran down deep in their burrows.

Skunk stood up laughing. The scent of roasted prairie dogs made Coyote drool and he suggested foot race to see who got choice pieces. At first Skunk said no, that it would not be fair because Coyote was too fast. Skunk only agreed after Coyote tied a rock to one foot. Coyote gave Skunk a head start. When Skunk was far ahead, he hid. Coyote started off slowly. After a short while he kicked off the stone and quickly passed the spot where Skunk was hidden.

Skunk went back to the fire and gathered all of the roast prairie dogs and carried the food into his brush pile. He was a better trickster than coyote that day.

Coyote and the Spying Moon

Someone had stolen the moon, and Coyote offered to replace him and the people elected him to the position. All the people agreed that he made a good moon.

From his lofty station Coyote could see everything and everybody. He could not resist announcing the deeds of his neighbors.

"Look what Squirrel is doing behind his tree!"

"See Badger sneaking into his neighbor's brush pile!"

After a while the people had had enough of his snooping and voted him out of the sky.

Then again, nothing can keep Coyote from doing just what he wants to do. He loves to impress the females by taking out his eyeballs and juggling them. Once he threw one so high that it got stuck in the sky. Now he's keeping an eye on everyone.

The Great Battle with Papawawe

Sinawava went hunting and killed two bear cubs. Their mother went to Papawawe (Bear) and demanded justice. A great battle began. Tivaci and Sinawava stood high on their mountain dressed in rainbow colors. Papawawe and his people advanced like a storm across the desert with lightning flashing from their lances, killing Tivaci and taking his hide. Sinawava tracked the bear tribe, finding them on the third day. He snuck into their camp, got inside his brother's hide, and scared all the bears away. Sinawava covered Tivaci's body with the hide and brought him back to life. Tivaci was alive, but very angry. Instead of returning home to their cave, Snow Having, Tivaci went north. This is why there are no wolves in Snow Having now.

CHAPTER 9

FLORA AND FAUNA

hidden life

Terry M. Mandeville

desert lives

cottontail hid motionless on white sand
of the desert land
nose twitched
he wished for a tender grass blade
or two
and maybe a vegetable garden to raid
cotton ball for a tail
he hopped down the trail like a child's stuffed toy

a black-tailed jackrabbit
cohabited the far side of the yard
long legs leapt and flew
a miniature kangaroo

in the wind the winged trickster soared
cawed and cried a high-pitched call
he would fly into the air

looney tune road runner, no wily in sight
atop the metal fence he darted in the moonlight
coyote, hare, tortoise, deer

browns and tans, colors of desert sands
yucca and cacti spread across the land
endless blue sky with sunset orange bands

We share the desert with a plethora of fellow creatures. Our friends the coyotes wander over the trails, zig-zagging across their territory. They are not the only creatures here. The ancient giant tortoises are hiding, buried deep into sunbaked sands for the winter. Rattlers are rather slow and hide out this time of year, but have made an appearance from time to time. There is one that lives in the rocks below the Joshua Tree National Park sign at the 29 Palms entrance.

Luna is especially interested in the lizards that scurry about under her nose. They are such fun sport, even though she never really catches them. She sticks her snout under the creosote bushes and down the burrows of the desert iguanas, snuffling the scent, and imagining what it would be like to play with the beings that hide deep within. Ever the mighty and brave hunter, she tracks the fence lizards across the rocks, the horned lizards across the sandy spots, and the spiny lizards among the Joshua trees.

Southern mule deer are skittish around humans and tend to stay away from the touristy spots. Sporting branched antlers and long mulish ears, I spy a buck guarding his doe harem in Covington Flats. He is sleek and handsome, soft brown, with big brown eyes. As I quietly approach for a photo, they catch my scent and bound rapidly away, hopping through the rough ground with all four hooves hitting the ground at the same time. A herd of bighorn sheep, with their curled horns, tread along the steep rocky ridges below Ryan Pass in the park eating the grasses and cacti.

Small desert wood rats are all over Black Rock, and the antelope ground squirrel scurries around Keys Point. I have never seen any tarantulas nor the glowing scorpions, probably because they tend to come out at night. Of all the rodents, Luna prefers the tiny pocket mice to sniff out as they hide in crevices around the yard. Those oh so cute kangaroo rats, their big round eyes, puffed cheeks, and huge feet make them look like little cartoon characters. They are great leapers, and very difficult to catch.

A blur of jackrabbit, seen but not heard, crosses the open space. Black-tailed jackrabbits, called "jackasses" by white settlers because their huge ears resemble a donkey's ear, bound across the yard and drive Luna into a frenzy. They have extremely efficient ears, like the yucca spines, up, up, straight up, ending in a point. The exposed surface of the ears helps them cool down in the desert heat and hear the tiniest sound. Their jumper legs help them hop like little mini kangaroos with blinding speed at about 40 miles per hour from a standing start. They can leap up to 10 feet high.

"Flopsy," "Mopsy" and "Cottontail" jump around the scene in little fast hops, then freeze like statues at the slightest hint of a threat. They are such cute, fluffy little bunnies; like cuddly stuffed animals. Tails like the cotton balls in a medicine bottle. Silent cottontail scurries from the brush, and freezes when he sees Luna. They have a silent staring contest for a few minutes. Then he hops away and Luna goes crazy.

I am not a bird-watcher. In spite of this, I find myself intrigued with them here. They are everywhere, a multitude of calls. A covey of Gambel's Quail scurries out from the brush at the side of the road, crossing in single file, little top notches bobbing to-and-fro. To the left a bit, no to the right; always keeping in perfect line. A cactus wren flits down the sand, staccato, pecking a pointed beak between the grains of sand. She is always wary of bigger creatures. Red-tailed hawks soar effortlessly on the wind. Whistles of the Scott's Oriole and the quiet trills of the logger head shrikes fill the air. Owls fly the night, and sometimes I see them hunting insects during the day. The green and purple Costa's Hummingbirds flit in for a visit. Up the hill, under the brush, a pair of mourning doves hide. They flush when this human gets too close. They call "coo, ah-wooo, cuck-ooo, oooo-oooo, oo-ooo-hoo."

Coyotes are not the only trickster here. Ravens, "flying tricksters," are old friends of mine. Coal black, like India ink. Squawking, they call out and sing to each other from the trees above. Teasing, warning, playing, taunting; they swoop, hop, perch, then fly away to scope out some new vantage point. "Caw, caw, caw." These scavengers scout for a meal; road kill or the bones of some other creature's dinner. They cry and flock and swoon in the scraggly pines. They watch, seeing all. Old jesters, they laugh a cosmic joke only the ravens know. Black shadows in the sun, smooth glistening wings. These new creatures called humans are their amusement.

Zigzagging to avoid predators, the sleek roadrunner darts across the scene on her long bare legs. She looks and acts not at all like her cartoon representation. This cuckoo bird certainly does not say "meep-meep," she coos like a dove. The roadrunner's call is supposed to make the listener feel tired. Brown and white streaked, she has a helmet-like crest on the top of her head and four toes, two facing forward and two facing backward. She is fast, even with no Wiley Coyote in pursuit, no Acme anvils hanging above, no cliffs to jump off. She doesn't fly well; yet she can easily get up into the tree to tease Luna.

After dark, lounging in the hot tub and watching the billions of stars, bats wing silently through the night above me. I catch them from the corner of my eye, black on black, but when I look, I can never see them clearly.

Teddy-bear cholla is a fuzzy looking, pretty bush. Sage green, looking all cuddly and warm. These beautiful, graceful works of art sprouting out of the desert sands, have maliciously spiteful stickers. Wicked weapons, harpooning hooks, stabbing spikes, they attack without warning, embedding deep in bare feet and dog noses. They can launch on the wind into unsuspecting flesh. In contrast, the delicate skeletons they leave behind when they die are smooth and beautiful. Lacy looking desert driftwood waiting to be gathered and pieced into art.

Creosote bushes surround me. They are amazing adaptations with their fragrant, yellow flowers. Among the oldest lifeforms on earth, some of these bushes are 12,000 years old and still flourish. They have chemicals in their roots that inhibit the growth of other plants so that the creosote bushes have more access to the scant available water. The leaves are waxy, which prevents the evaporation of moisture.

Although not as lush as that of the pacific northwest, there are many other varieties of vegetation, indigenous as well as visitors from elsewhere. Juniper, pinyon pines, barrel cacti, prickly pear, fan palm, ocotillo, and varieties of yucca. Smaller ground huggers take hold in shaded dips and undisturbed spots. After a rain. little patches of green grass appear.

Terry M. Mandeville

desert flora

quiet of winter desert
dry and bold
browns and golds
life with stories to be told
so many wonders to behold

stark primal joshua trees as one
reaching toward distant sun
channeling with cool of season
just begun
anticipating potential rains
where there has been none

life under blue of sky
white puffy clouds lie below the sun
frigid winds making sands fly
swirl around the dry land

CHAPTER 10
ALIENS, UFOS AND STRANGE
STUFF

welcome

Terry M. Mandeville

travelers

these twisted trees
stark walls of granite
could very well greet
travelers from other planets
who would see?

aliens here on a road trip
never dislodged
from their buried spaceships
in the mojave
who hides their secrets?

have they listened and adjusted?
watched and roamed?
influenced and discussed?
sent messages back home?
who is one among us?

My search for self, for inner quiet, would not be complete without exploring the other-worldly properties of the whole area, especially Landers, a spread-out community in the middle of the high desert just uphill from JT. The area is ablaze with UFO sightings, alien-themed settings, cosmic vibes, and strange tales.

Ancient tribes said that this area of the Mojave Desert is comprised of high energy vortexes that magnify anything inside. The natives believe that earth's energy can amplify the emotional, spiritual, physical, or mental. This is why the land is sacred to them. The national park has 18 known vortices on the land. These vortexes are said to help those who seek a closer connection with a supreme being, divine assistance, healing, inspiration, or creativity.

I wander down the loose sand road that snakes to a monolith called Giant Rock. I have to drive slowly for the potholed, jiggly washboard of a road. Way out in the middle of nowhere I arrive at a seven-story freestanding boulder near Landers, allegedly the largest freestanding boulder in America, if not the world. Native Americans have long considered it to be a sacred site. The Hopi would celebrate the coming seasons here with tribes from across the desert. Shamans are drawn to the rock to gain spiritual strength for their tribe. The magic in the rock is said to represent "the heart of Mother Earth." It is an area where people have been drawn for spiritual energy since ancient times. I am sad to see that, in this remote setting, vandals have tagged the rock and graffiti indelicately litters the scene.

Like many things in the Mojave, this has a further twisted and strange history. In the 1930s a prospector named Frank Critzer dug out a large single room beneath the gigantic rock. He set up house there, inspired by the desert tortoises who bury themselves in the sand in summer to cool down, and in winter to stay warm. He built a rainwater collection system and a ventilation tunnel. During World War II he was suspected of being a German spy because of his interest in radios and his elaborate antennae system on his rock. He was killed during a law enforcement raid on his cave. Some stories claim that a tear gas canister thrown by the agents ignited his store of dynamite. No one knows the truth. The burned-out abode was closed and locked for years, and they say that all of Critzer's possessions were removed by the government.

The rock is located on land which was subsequently leased from the government by George Van Tassel, a friend of Mr. Critzer's. Van Tassel was an engineer and former test pilot for Howard Hughes. He developed the Giant Rock Airport and a Café. Van Tassel held weekly meditations in the room under the rock and the surrounding area from the 1950s to the 1970s. Thousands of UFO believers, electromagnetic researchers, antigravity seekers, and energy researchers attended his conventions every year.

Because of these gatherings, Van Tassel claimed that he was contacted by a flying-saucer and given directions on how to build a "rejuvenation and time machine," with the intention of generating electricity to "charge the human body" and extend life. These "UFO channelings," and ideas from scientists such as Nikola Tesla, led to his design of the Integratron, a 38-foot-tall wooden structure. The building site was deemed ideal because the earth's magnetic field is strong near Giant Rock's crystalline structure. The Integratron was built according to the aliens' directions. This 16-sided dome built of wood and concrete, is held together with wooden dowels, glue and "gravity-electrically neutral materials."

Eighteen years into the project Van Tassel unexpectedly died of a heart attack. The "rejuvenation" portion was left unfinished. Much of the mechanism of the rejuvenation machine disappeared mysteriously. Van Tassel's family eventually abandoned the site and now it has become the scene for Sound Baths because of its mystical properties and the remarkable acoustics of the structure, even without the lost longevity mechanism.

Hopi shaman reportedly had prophesized that the future of the 21st century could be foretold at Giant Rock. If the rock split in half Mother Earth was disillusioned with humankind. If the rock split on the side, then prayers would be answered, ushering in a new era. In March of 2000 it was discovered that a third of the enormous granite rock had split and slid off, exposing a shining white interior. Many theories were born. Had the Hopi prophecy been fulfilled? Was this a demonstration of alien power? Is there a disruption in the earth's magnetic field? Is the date that the rock split, 0324-2000, an encrypted message? Did the government stage the event in order to remove evidence of alien presence?

Despite the nearness of the Marine Base, and several small airports, there have been many UFO sightings in the Joshua Tree area. Many. In June of 2016 JT held a "Contact in the Desert UFO Conference." On June 4th, during the conference as attendees were stargazing, many reported witnessing multiple UFOs. There were said to be multi-colored orbs, bright blue and orange, hovering overhead. These orbs supposedly created different formations, ultimately creating a triangle. Other sightings have been reported over the years.

You can spend a night in a UFO in JT. An orange, spaceship-shaped structure, the "Futuro House," is set in "Area 55" on the slopes north of JT. There are only 68 known Futuro Houses in the world, and this is the only one in the USA that you can spend the night in. I have considered it, but it is rather pricey, even for one night.

Perhaps the most difficult, and strange, structure to fathom in JT itself are the remnants of a fictional cabin. Yes, a "fictional" cabin! Krblin Jihn's cabin is the fictional spot where Jihn of Kcymaerxthaere, a fictional alternative universe, was to have lived. Bizarre as it seems, there really is a structure there, a prop so to speak, a physical illustration of the novel.

Skinwalkers, known as "yee naaldlooshii" by the Hopi natives for hundreds of years, are said to inhabit the Mojave Desert. These are supposed to be witches who have the ability to turn themselves into animals. These animals are usually the tricksters, such as Coyote, but also owls, foxes or wolves. They are believed to hunt humans.

Desert Dungeon is a cave with an iron door that was found in the desert. Although no one really knows its history, there have been many reports of it being used as a prison. One common theory is that a man used it to imprison his horribly disfigured son. The son is said to have broken out and terrorizes the surrounding area even today.

Another weird tale is of Yucca Man, a Sasquatch-like creature that has been reported in the area. A Marine guard on duty at the base in 29 was discovered unconscious with his rifle bent in half. The soldier reported that he was attacked by a 12-foot-tall hairy man who grabbed his rifle, bent it, and knocked him unconscious. Others have reported encounters with "a man the size of a refrigerator," with long arms. The man was said to be covered in long, tan hair.

Stories of ghosts and spiritual apparitions are common. The ghost of Gram Parsons, father of country rock, has appeared to some in room 8 of the Joshua Tree Inn, where he died in 1973. There are reported to be a high number of missing persons and unexplained deaths in the Joshua Tree area. Some spots in the desert are so isolated and secluded, yet close enough to the city, that they seem perfect for secret disposal of bodies. It is also inevitable that unprepared visitors wander far out into the desert and succumb to the heat and lack of water. It is an unforgiving environment that can easily lead to death.

There are many stories of strange happenings in the Mojave, and Joshua Tree National Park in particular. Hikers feeling watched from something hidden. Encounters with crazy-looking people acting strangely. Eerie sounds. Symbols drawn in the sand, painted on buildings, or built out of objects.

Another cosmic place way out in the middle of nowhere is "On God's Way Love Road: Garth's Boulder Gardens." It is a private 640-acre eco-friendly spiritual retreat area in the middle of the desert amid huge boulders and rock formations near Pioneertown. Garth Bowles spent many decades molding this spot, and it continues in his memory to this day.

To many, the unbelievable structure known as the Cosmic Castle is the focal point of the Boulder Gardens. It sits upon a huge boulder and the walls inside are made of earth materials and murals. An ancient pinion pine tree grows up through the castle, making it look like a cement treehouse. Several windows with carved frames show off views of the 100-mile-long Pipes

Canyon. The exterior is cement, made to look like a boulder sitting on a boulder. A decorated narrow cement stairway winds up and around the tree and boulder to the door.

Other structures inside the gardens include a cement tipi, a wood-burning sauna, fish ponds, bird aviaries, a pool, an amphitheater, a yoga deck, open air caves, old sofas and chairs, a "wine cellar," and an outdoor kitchen. Crystals and rocks litter the tables, alters, and are laid out in patterns around trees. There are a variety of animals including snakes, bullfrogs, peacocks, chickens and roosters, squirrels, quail, desert turtles, rabbits, lizards, and a variety of dogs. Water is supplied by year-round springs and several ponds. Fruit trees, Joshua trees and cacti grow, and there are petroglyphs. Garth hand laid 3 1/2 miles of piping to bring water from the solar-powered well, up 300 feet in elevation. At Garth's Boulder Gardens there is always music, drumming, and there is even a grand piano. Garth's mesmerizing stories are carried on by his tribe. If it sounds hippie-ish, counterculture, and trippy – it is! And yes, some people do partake of recreational drugs while there.

For me, the vibes in the desert are soothing and positive. I refuse to label it. I don't want to analyze it. It is what it is. If creatures from another place in the universe are guiding me here, so be it. It doesn't seem sinister. I will take all of the desert's gifts gratefully.

strong medicine

earth mother is close here
the shamans were led here
drawn here

drawn toward the power of the mystical sovarampi
the healing medicine of the golden sands
the towering strength of the rocks
the spiritual essence of the land

fulfilling prophesy
comforting, nurturing, healing
the force of nature
revealing

Terry M. Mandeville

opening

been hunkered down so long
protecting
not letting the light through
walls i build each day anew

been closed
hard nosed
solitary
exercising my will
very sad and very still

been keeping protected
dejected
rejecting souls that come my way

then i found myself a warm spot
in the desert, I melted into the sand
slowly opened my mind
open my hands
up to the blue sky

opened like petals of spring flowers
busting down walls
feeling myself fall
into me

CHAPTER 11

INSIDE THE PARK

mystic lands

Terry M. Mandeville

finding quiet in the park

snaking toward the hills
i join the weekend throng
the lookie-loos
the weekend tourists coming along

they stand mid-road
looking to see
a sign of something wild
finding quiet in the park is not easy

full parking lots
loaded rv pulls
people sitting inside their vehicles
with the ac on full

Again the desert sky is clear. I am behind a string of vehicles travelling up Park Boulevard, all with the same purpose in mind. We are going into the park, waiting our turn to show our passes to enter at the gate. Once released, we begin the parade around the backbone of hills that line the valley with craggy rock.

Joshua Tree National Park has been "discovered." Most of the time a long line of cars wait to enter, especially on weekends in the spring or fall. Parking lots fill up fast. Tourists stop mid-road to gawk, everyone with camera in hand. It seems that most visitors take it slow, treasure the natural beauty and abide by the park rules. I am upset by the few that manage to maneuver their vehicles off road, past boulders purposely put in place to prevent such careless ventures, to endanger the health and lives of the fragile Joshua trees and other vegetation.

Indeed, the park gets its name from the spiny yucca trees, but there is far more to explore here. It is a huge place, about the size of Rhode Island, much of it inaccessible by vehicle. There are hills and mountain ranges inside the park: Cottonwood, Little San Bernardino, Pinto, Eagle, Hexie, and Coxcomb Mountains. They are separated by valleys. The entrance road goes up and curves for miles around the hills, rocks and outcroppings of the Mojave. Craggy boulders morph into polished monoliths surrounded by forests of Joshua trees stretching to the bordering mesas and hills. I marvel at each sculptured rock I see as they appear, one after another. Each different, each spectacular. I could gaze at these monoliths forever still find new sights, continually in awe, never bored.

The road wanders past crowded campgrounds, bustling trailheads, remarkable viewpoints, narrow rock canyons, pointy yucca, impossible stacks of boulders, glittering sands, and legendary iconic formations.

Joshua Tree National Park (JTNP) contains two different deserts and three different ecosystems. The southeastern portion of the park consists of the Colorado Desert, which is a western extension of the Sonoran Desert.

The northern portion of the park contains the southern part of the Mojave Desert. The western ecosystem of JTNP is an area higher than 4000 feet above sea level.

Most visitors to the park cluster around the big boulder areas not too far inside the main northern entrance. Split and Intersection Rocks are enormous boulders with cracks that run from bottom to top, speckled with rock climbers. Other rocks are miraculous balancing acts. Cap Rock is an unbelievable vision with a massive flat rock teetering atop a huge boulder. Arch Rock is a curved archway that spans over 30 feet in a slot canyon. Nearby is Heart Rock, a perfect heart-shaped boulder over 10 feet tall, that was a well-kept secret for years. Parking is at a premium near Skull Rock, which looks like a creepy gigantic skull with two sunken eye sockets. It is an amusing stop. Hidden Valley, Hall of Horrors, and Jumbo Rocks are all exhibitions of nature as the artist omnipotent. An ancient juniper tree arches over towards the huge Penguin Rock that resembles a penguin.

There are ancient forces here. Cold water and wind have sculpted and shaped these rocks, hammered by the elements. The San Andreas Fault system, which goes 700 miles from the Gulf of California to the Mendocino Coast north of San Francisco, runs underground just outside the park. Tons of rock are inching past each other under there.

Keys View allows the perfect spot from the top of the Little San Bernadino Mountains to observe the fault. You can see where it branches off into two smaller faults with a chunk of black rock, the Indigo Hills, between them. Down a mile from the ridge are views of Coachella Valley. The Salton Sea can be seen shimmering to the far left. To the right is Indio and Palm Springs, with the Santa Rosa Mountains and Jacinto Peak behind them. To the far right is the 11,500-foot San Gorgonio Mountain. If there is no smog, they say you can see Signal Mountain in Mexico.

In the Barker Dam area there is a giant overhanging boulder which is home to some petroglyphs. 2000-year-old dark yellow and black desert varnish of manganese, iron, and clays coats many of the rocks. The ancient petroglyphs have been carved into this varnish. Only the well protected ones have survived and are still visible.

Eventually I send dust trails that puff behind the truck as I drive off the main pavement. This is my secret quiet place. Geology Tour Road, a sand road that is not too popular. It is an 18-mile unpaved road that eventually could take me to the Cottonwood Oasis if I wanted, near the southern entrance to the park. After the first six miles, however, it becomes deeply rutted with tilted granite alternating with soft sand. It requires a high clearance four-wheel drive vehicle. Now although my little red truck does satisfy that requirement, it is not something I really desire to attempt alone, especially since the interior of the park does not have reliable cell phone service. The upper area is flat. The outcroppings of rock are fascinating. Several turn outs near the poorly travelled road provide quiet spaces for writing with Luna on her tie-out.

I open my folding chair to a mess of stink bugs that must have hitched a ride from home. I shake them out, they are catatonic in this chill and will probably die in the freeze at night. I worry for a moment about introducing an invasive species to the desert, then I remember that stink bugs are native here too. Oh, even though the sun is out and it is a blue, blue sky, it is cold in January here. I bundle in my down coat and hood, blanket covering my legs, oversized sunglasses to shade the sun's glare. I breathe, I sigh, I observe, I dream, I write. Animals have dug and clawed homes under the shrubs all around me, and Luna is in Seventh Heaven nosing after them. Finally, I must stop writing when I can't feel my fingers any more. Pack up the truck and move on. Back to the tourists and the pavement.

Backtracking, I pull into the Ryan Mountain parking lot for the view. You never know what you are going to see next in the ongoing movie here. Sculptured rock, twisted vegetation, big horned sheep. Hikers, families, rock climbers ...nuns. I interject myself a bit into the desert and set out my chair in the winter sun for a second time, bundled yet again in my fluffy purple down parka against the chill wind.

Can't go too far because again Luna, the desert dog, is with me and not allowed on the trails. She is on her long leash tie out again and she is content to move in circles, exploring the smells and sounds. My favorite pen and the yellow notebook are in my lap, and the parade begins. Assorted rainbows of people begin to sparkle in the sun.

Eventually the main road splits. One fork winds back around and down into town at 29 Palms. The other travels down, down, down into the flat of the Colorado desert. The road passes the spiny fields of Teddy Bear cholla at the Cholla Gardens, healthy and sprouting pretty bright yellow cup-like remnants of blossoms. The gardens are where everyone stops to take more photos, and utter "ohhh" and "ahhhh," and a few "ouches" as they brush too close. Just beyond is the Ocotillo Patch. The road crosses miles through the low desert, and straight on through the barren landscape to the sudden lush Cottonwood Oasis, disappearing as quickly as it appears. The road finally emerges at a desolate, non-descript exit onto Highway 10.

There are other areas of the park that are accessed from the perimeters and not obvious to the casual tourist. Approached from the northern edge of the park are Black Rock Canyon, Indian Cove, and Canyon Road with its trailhead to the thriving 49 Palms Oasis. These are beautiful areas but they do not allow one to drive deep into the park proper. Here I find remote trails and roads, campgrounds, Nature Centers and lots of flora and fauna.

Covington Flats is another uncrowded area off the beaten track. It is found from a kind of hidden and mostly unsupervised entry into the park in the north-western part, between Black Rock Canyon and JT. The sand roads in the flats, and above, are entirely unpaved and contain portions of very loose sand. They traverse some of the park's largest, and oldest, Joshua trees, junipers, and pinyon pines. I feel safe in my high-clearance truck, with four-wheel drive, I haven't needed the four-wheel drive yet though. There are many trails in the area. It is great for biking, off-roading, and the scenery. I have seen deer and coyote there.

Going to Eureka Peak at the end of the Covington Flats Road, the road is reasonably well maintained, with a few rough and sandy spots, and it gets steep at the end. The sand can get kind of deep in a few spots, and "wash-boarded" after a rain. It is worth it, though, because the top presents spectacular views of Palm Springs, the San Bernardino and the Santa Rosa Mountains, and the Morongo Basin rivalling Keys View. It's better than Keys View because it's not crowded. The peak is the fourth highest summit in the park, after Quail Mountain, Queen Mountain, and Inspiration Peak. It is 5472 feet above sea level.

The park has 57 different mammal species. Ravens and other birds are common. Bigger animals stay away from humankind if they can. Snakes and kangaroo rats are often seen at the Black Rock and Covington Flats areas. Big horned sheep sometimes frequent Ryan Mountain.

Back home I am happy in my native national parks: Rainier, Olympic, North Cascades. They are majestic, peaceful and comforting. JTNP has something else though.

There is a mystical quality here. Its many "energy vortices" are said to be akin to chakras in the practice of yoga. Many believe that JTNP is "one of the most powerful and energetic places in the world." The forces of the "vortex" in this spiritual, ancient place is said to magnify everything we humans bring with us into the park. Our emotions, our spiritual plain, our physical attributes and our mental abilities are all said to be amplified. This park has always been about finding peace.

magic place

this magic place
blues of sky
with white puffy clouds
that lie
below the sun

the wind comes up slowly
making sands fly
building with towering intensity
now with definite power spins the land dry

i find my spot
in the chill winter wind
that mocks the desert
sucking all the warmth from within

Terry M. Mandeville

joshua trees blossom

field of joshua tree
stretch across high flats
infinite horizon seen
to craggy habitat

a forest of shape
like a garden of gargoyles
twisted lines gape
up from desert soil

they smile
having just drunk
from the winter rain a while
water coursing up along their trunks

they will bloom
pushing forth fisted buds of green
soon
creamy snow cone of blossoms seen

moths and squirrels
will feast on the bounty
and life will go on and circle
all around me

CHAPTER 12

LIVING IN THE MOJAVE

who the heck saw this place and said
"man, what a cool and practical place
to live?"

Terry M. Mandeville

camping between the rocks

campfire reflected on the clean white rock wall
crackling, flickering, magical
tents nestle right against rock for shade
for shelter from the wind or rain

we spread out for all to see
settle out in the air
sand in our eyes, our hair
sand seasoning our food
gritting our teeth
scouring our tender skin
warming under bare feet
scraping in our boots
itching in our beds
sifting inside everything
gritty, embedded

canvas for the campfire
you see tents rise from the floor
in reds, blues, yellows, greens
colors startle in the desert
backdrop for our state of mind
in the desert you can't hide

The village of JT is a unique mix of cultures. Only 2 ½ hours from LA, less than an hour from Palm Springs, it is a totally different world. Even the next-door towns of Yucca and 29 differ profoundly. Residents in JT make up a happy group of old hippies, sculptors, persons of the LGBTQ+ community, rock climbers, painters, desert rats, psychedelic aficionados, retired tourists, gurus, acoustic musicians, assemblage artists, and other diverse people. Intermingled, included, appreciated. A wonderfully blended eclectic mix. It is a place I feel comfortable in my jeans and t-shirt, with no makeup, hair undone, and no explanation needed. No pretense. No games.

It is Saturday and I am going to the Joshua Tree Farmer's Market, it is more or less a local street fair. It's only open in the morning, so I have to get going early. I join the throng of people, babies and dogs as they stroll among the colorful stalls of crafts, vegetables, fruits, flowers, and other foods. A busker plays his guitar and sings at the end of the street, and he is quite good!

Terry M. Mandeville

White tents punctuate the parking lot next to art museums, gift shops, and organic restaurants. First stop, the microgreens for some sunflower sprouts and spicy mix. Everyone is giving out free samples and, like at Costco, one could probably lunch on the munchies.

Next, I browse through all the different vegetable stands, amazed at what is growing in the winter here. I pick between organic, fresh and local oranges, broccoli, spinach, lettuces, yams, cabbages, asparagus, cherries, raspberries, peppers, onions, garlic, strawberries, apples, kale, and herbs.

A variety of rainbow-colored carrots, beets, tomatoes, cauliflower and potatoes. There are tempting cheeses, eggs, pastries, honey, homemade jam, almonds, pistachios, teas, coffee, salsas, and pickled things. I should have known better than to come hungry! I talk with the fisherman selling smoked salmon, cod and halibut about fishing off the coast of Alaska.

The artist who makes sparkling Joshua tree necklaces is from the Pacific Northwest, so we share a bit about home and the differences here. There are soaps and candles of desert aromas, and lots of other jewelry. I commiserate with the man selling borscht about the war in Ukraine. The vendor selling tubs of dolma yells something at me in Greek, and I smile because I have not a clue what he said.

A sunny Saturday is crowded in the village of JT, doesn't matter what time of year it is. Tourists and locals get in line at the Crossroads Café for a late breakfast. They say the wait will be 30 minutes. It's more like an hour. I finally get a spot at the counter and, now that it is lunch time, quickly order a beer with my Crossroads omelet. The waitress laughs that only a local would order a beer with breakfast. I ask the young cashier about his REI t-shirt, which leads to a discussion about leading hikes and teaching rock climbing in the park.

Next, I duck into The Dez Fine Food for some salads to take home. The clerk is singing in Palm Springs tonight and I get details. I know I am probably not going to drive that far and back in the dark, but I am interested to know about her musical achievements.

Many of the buildings in JT exhibit an old west motif; storefronts are wooden or adobe replicas from old cowboy movies. The saloon, cafes, odd museums, shops, repurposed art and clothing exist side by side with clusters of Joshua trees. Josh, the tall cowboy statue, beckons visitors into The Station, an old gasoline station made into a gift shop. There are several abandoned shops and houses along the main highway through the village. I wonder who lived there, who had businesses there, and why they left.

On other days I frequent the Joshua Tree Saloon. Now this institution is not just a bar and grill. It is a destination. In all its cowboy glory the saloon beckons. Old West murals adorn the outside stone walls. Inside are old wooden floors and a long bar backed by rows and rows of bottles filled with many colors of liquid. There is a little stage in the corner set up with all manner of equipment, ready for the weekend of free music. A pool table with faded green felt is shoved in an alcove by the old main door off the highway. No one is shooting pool today. Photos of '60s rock stars dot the walls, along with old license plates, cowboy hats, t-shirts, posters and stained glass.

Outside in the courtyard are scattered tables and benches amid antique cars, mining equipment and gasoline pumps. Parked out the back, which is now the main entrance for some unknown reason, and around the parking lots are several old hippie busses. They had been outfitted as abodes for road trips at one time, with tattered tie-dyed curtains and faded psychedelic colors. They now are apparently used for storage.

Breakfast at the saloon used to come with a side of the best little German potato pancakes in the world, like my mother used to make. After Covid shutdown breakfast at the saloon, it is unfortunately a thing of the past. Luckily the fantastic fish and chips paired with a "Happy Hippie" or a "Cowgirl Gunslinger" cocktail makes me happy.

The Joshua Tree Brewery is "temporarily" closed as they find a new local venue. Sad, because it was a fun place to hang out in the evening outside amid the twinkling lights. The sage and lavender beer, made in honor of the rock climbers in the village, was unique and delicious.

Coyote Corner is a little old wooden gift shop known the world over. Used to be able to get a shower outside, $5 for seven and a half minutes. During Covid, the line to get in the store stretched out the door, across the porch and around the corner, six at a time inside. Racks of recycled clothes for a bargain hang on the porch just outside the door. Inside is a fascinating eclectic combination of wares.

There are many other funky gift shops along the highway in JT, 29 and Yucca. More pop up starting in February along the Art Queen strip off the highway near the Saloon. The National Park Gift Shop, the Rock Shop, and Rainbow Stew are more permanent fixtures with everything from local art, crystals, jewelry, clothing, trinkets, books, and all kinds of souvenirs.

Lots of yummy food in the area, and I eat out often. Sam's Pizza and Indian Food is always packed. The Country Kitchen, with its long line of people hanging about the sidewalk for brunch and mimosas, is a must. The local caffeine fix, Joshua Tree Coffee, is unparalleled. Just next door is Sky High Pizza with unique pizza combinations and great beer. I must also mention that the Rib Co, although in 29, features mouthwatering fare, grilled right out in front of the restaurant. That is saying something, as I usually don't much like barbeque.

The village and the surrounding vicinity are an orderly grid of sand roads, many appear to lead nowhere. Most roads go straight on. They don't deviate around dips or trees, and only dead end at mountains, deep ravines or cliffs.

JT village itself is not the only town in the area. Nearby towns are each a different little pocket of culture. Each unquestionably having its own vibe, its own character, its own kind of people.

Yucca is the big town next to JT. It has a Walmart, big grocery stores, a couple of Dollar Stores, car dealerships, real estate offices, fast food and restaurants, a bowling alley, medical clinics, and many strange and unique pairings. "Old Town" Yucca has the eclectic Frontier Café, for vegan stuff and coffee, and lots of funky little gift and antique stores. It is errand day and I have to do my grocery shopping here because JT only has little mom and pop stores.

The place seems like a little town trying to be a bigger city with an odd combination of small new strip malls, old abandoned movie theaters, faded signs in front of long forgotten establishments, and restaurants that seem to frequently move from place to place. It hosts prayer meetings with the mayor, swim in movies, flying doctors medical clinic, and "no snow play on the roadway" signs.

An old drive-in movie theater in Yucca has been turned into the Sky Village Swap Meet. It is an outdoor bazaar. Nestled in the middle of the Sky Village is Bob's Crystal Cave made of thousands of crystals and gems; amethysts, rose quartz, seashells and porcelain. It even has a little waterfall. The cave was begun to inspire people and make a place of love and meditation.

Right on the main highway thru Yucca is the Dog and Car Wash. Nozzled hoses dangle from the shiny tiled walls. What a concept! My imagination has me driving the truck in, with Luna in the bed, and spraying down both at once. Is there wax spray for the dog's coat? Detangler for the truck antenna? Scratch remover for Luna's claws? Flea spray to keep the kangaroo rats from the engine?

Further to the west and down the hill a bit towards Palm Springs, Morongo Valley looks like just a leveled off spot-on highway 62 with a couple of stoplights and gas stations on the way from the low to the high desert. There are massive public lands for hiking, and ranches with horseback riding. Fellow Earthlings Wildlife Center is a meercat sanctuary nearby, but one basically has to "adopt a meerkat" for $400 to be able to visit.

29 is along highway 62 on the other side, the east side of JT. You hit the newer western part of the small town, the grocery stores and a few hotels, and then think that's all there is when you come up against the hill. Up and over the hill; you come to the old part of town lined with lots of Mexican restaurants, art museums, small stores, military themed displays, and murals. The city was named for the 29 palm trees

that were found there by the first white surveyor in the area. The Serrano originally settled it. They called it Mara, meaning "the place of little springs and much grass." Their tales say that they came to the oasis when their shaman directed them to come. He told them to plant a palm tree each time a boy was born. In the first year, the Serrano planted 29 palm trees at the oasis.

The original source of water and activity was the Oasis of Mara which is divided into two parts. The east side of the oasis has a long strip of palm trees that border the East Entrance JTNP Visitor's Center. There is a sidewalk trail around the trees. The oasis has suffered from drought and wildfires in recent years. On the west side the oasis, with a large beautiful pond surrounded by date palms, is owned by the historic 29 Palms Inn and has a great restaurant.

The large Marine Corps Air Ground Combat Center is just to the north and colors much of the city's activities, including the Tortoise Rock Casino in the tiny reservation of the Twenty-Nine Palms Band of Mission Indians.

Pioneertown, population 511, is up the hill north of Yucca. Named for the Sons of the Pioneers, it is mainly known as an old film set for old westerns. Now-a-days it is a cowboy themed town with gift shops, saloons, motel, and a movie museum. Roy Rogers, Gene Autry and the Sons of the Pioneers all frequented the area at one time. Several old movies and TV shows, including the Cisco Kid, were shot there and they have an old west show on the weekend during tourist season. Pioneertown is also the setting for Pappy and Harriet's, a bar and grill that was a former biker bar called "The Cantina." It was at one time a stage where western movies were made. It is now a very popular concert venue.

As twisted as the Joshua trees themselves, the structures of the desert are unique and individual. No tract housing, no "ticky-tacky" here. Warm colored stucco blends like the sand itself rising from the earth to form shelter, rising to the red tiled rooftops like sunrise, like the heat, the fire. Here and there tiny wooden houses are painted bright unnatural shades that startle, sparkle, bringing color to the desert. Desert rats live here in old mining sheds. Old hippies in bedraggled "Jackrabbit" huts painted in bright pinks and neon blue, murals on the walls of coyote, fauna, flora. Shipping containers, cut and welded together, form unusual houses. Tumble down shacks that have baked in the sun a bit too long. Repurposed materials made into homes of windows and sky lights. Mirrored mansions that hide amid the rocks. Western ranches. Hippie tipis. Cave dwellings. Remodeled sheds. Sod shelters. Curved labyrinths. Antique Airstream Trailers. UFO shaped residences. Plywood cabins. Military barracks. Rock lodgings built into the boulders. Tree houses.

Unsurprisingly, artists and architects have been drawn to this area for decades. They have designed and built many unique homes incorporating the lines and beauty of the desert. Artists can rent sci-fi pods in the rocks at Andrea Zittel's "Wagon Station Encampment." The "High Desert House" is organic architecture that looks like a skeleton from a distance. Three sculptured outdoor bedrooms make up "Seasonal Pavilions." "Joshua Tree Residence" is a clustered assemblage of shipping containers. A remodeled abandoned homestead called "Folly" consists of stainless-steel cabins that are off the grid.

Trailers, RVs and tents of all size and description are packed into the campgrounds. Campers under brightly colored nylon tents flutter against smooth rock boulders. Tents nestle right against rock, rise from the desert floor in reds, greens, blues, and yellows. Campfires are reflected in the clean white rock wall, crackling, flickering, magical. Shiny Silver Streak trailers sparkle on the sand, reflecting sun.

Around the houses Christmas lights are strung along patios and decks, lighting the darkness with dots of lights for humans who are afraid of the dark. A few mansions, two storied airconditioned retreats, create their own universes. Bright lights reach out into the night. Transplanted cacti from other deserts form a human terraformed oasis. Sand raked clean by the hired man, fenced away from the riff raff. Multi-colored pools reflect ripples of water, ripples of light onto the ripples of the sand.

Deserted tiny abodes litter the landscape; old "Jackrabbit" hovels from the 1940s. They cost five dollars each from the government, on five acres of land, and they had five years to build and live there. No water, no electricity. Homesteaders came in droves, built their little shacks, lived there for a while, then just as quickly abandoned it all. Now only empty cement or wooden walls are left, although a few have been remodeled and are rented out to tourists. Old houses are picked clean as the wind blows through missing doors and window panes, whittled and weathered by blowing sands, blistering heat, ice and cold. Skeletons of old miner's cabins, farmers shacks, very slowly melt into kibble.

My abode in the desert is above the village of JT. A place of solitude. A place of quiet. A place to write. I have met friendly neighbors of all ages, with dogs that play with Luna. I even have a hot tub here, something I don't have at home. Hot water surrounds me, bubbles between my toes. Relaxation has found me, sipping a margarita in bliss, majestic scenes in the distance. A water cocoon blankets me, hugs me, nurtures me, loves me.

The other day the lady at Dez's told me that she thought I was a native JT resident. Lord knows I feel like one. I feel natural here, at ease, family, home spun. I beam at the compliment. I am no longer a tourist, not an outcast. I know i am one with the desert at last, at least for now.

Terry M. Mandeville

little shops and saturday's market

in town on a saturday
shopping as the time slips away browsing all the displays
aromatic sachets and candles of scented bouquets
books on shamanism, humanism, altruism
crystals and prisms
bumper stickers with cacti and sunsets, joshua tree silhouettes
tortoises with jewels inset, refrigerator magnets
a relic painted psychedelic
camping and climbing kits, coyote statuettes
maps, straw hats, grateful dead caps, medicine
sacks, tie dyed wraps cactus candies, salts from the sea,
local cheddar and ricotta and brie
joshua tree seeds, pottery
spotted beans, rainbow of leafy salad greens,
many flavors of honey and teas scented oils and lotions
herbal potions, an old hippie bus time has frozen
red tomatoes, blue potatoes, avocados
globes that glow, basil and oregano
plants of aloe, a cup of joe
earrings of crystal, cacti that bristle, postcards and a whistle
colorful socks, crystals and rocks, woven bookmarks
art, hippie skirts, t-shirts
a bath house in the desert, a busker concert
cactus flower jams, bright orange yams
yellow daises and sunflowers
i browse for hours

CHAPTER 13

DESERT DOG

luna in the desert

Terry M. Mandeville

don't eat the cacti

lizards to track, ravens to envy their flight
rodents behind the fence, scents to take in at night
but luna you might die if you eat the cacti

sunshine to warm your fur, shade to cool the land
while you take a nap stretched out on the desert sand
but luna, i sigh, please don't eat the cacti

dreams that make you soar and twitch
bark and wine, growl and fidget
but luna, you cannot fly and you cannot eat the cacti

coyotes yip in the distance, you wake with tucked tail
comforted that i am still here with you
we protect one another as they wail
but luna, those coyotes lie when they tell you to eat the cacti

you explore again with your nose, the breeze is pleasant
with your mouth to taste the desert essence
but luna why would you want to eat cacti?

My dog is the perfect travel companion, as well as the perfect housemate. She settles in her crate in the truck and generally just goes with the flow, although she gets a little grumpy on curvy or washboard roads. If it's a full day of driving she lets me know when she is fed up with it and needs a break.

When we get where we are going, she is at home just about anywhere. I don't have to ask her which bed she wants, where to put things, or what to watch on the TV. She doesn't care if I leave dishes in the sink, or towels on the floor. We don't have disagreements over what to cook for dinner, although she does beg for the chicken every time I cook it. As long as she gets to run a bit, sniff around, eat when she's hungry, and get some kind words and attention she is happy. Of course, she doesn't have a job and never pays her share of the bills. She does perform her doggie chores of licking the dishes clean, guarding against critters, and barking at noises. She is content to have me as cook, companion, and housekeeper; to keep her warm or cool as needed, take her for walks, find other dogs to play with, and to share a bed at night.

Terry M. Mandeville

Luna loves the desert; the smells, the sounds, the moving sands, even the distant coyotes and ravens. She was rescued as a pup from a flood in Texas and she remains very fearful of water, so the desert suits her, although she is not a fan of extreme heat either. My spoiled diva friend thinks it wise that we are not here in the summer.

This sable and cream-colored dog blends with the sand. Camouflaged, she feels safe here. She pads silently, sniffing cautiously around the bush. Nose to the desert floor she tracks the aromatic trails and gingerly noses the burrows. She sticks her snout right into critter holes and yucca trunks, sniffing the lair.

She is at home in the desert. She stretches her long dog body on the warm sand; longer, longer as she stretches out to her full length. She is tall and slender and runs like a greyhound with a "double suspension gallop" (the hind legs follow the forelegs; all four feet leave the ground at the same time.) Her DNA shows her to be a curious blend of more than 15 different canine breeds, none of which look like her. She has no greyhound or whippet in her whatsoever. She drools like the mastiff in her lineage. Her ridgeback ancestry is why her hair stands up over her spine when she goes into defense mode. She hunts small scurrying things like the terrier in her. The pom in her created blue spots on her tongue and leads her to be affectionate. Her coloring is similar to her white lab ancestor. My Luna is her own unique being, with the best of all traits.

Squinting in the sun, she smiles. No rain on her fur to irritate her. No deep icy snow to freeze her paws. Open desert, she watches the sands as they roll, keenly aware of the ravens perched on the Joshua trees above as they squawk and caw. Raising her snout, she sniffs the desert air, long pulls into her lungs, and she smiles again as if it triggers some ancient memory in her doggie brain.

Deep breaths, she drinks the air. Smells of coyote on the wind, big horned sheep scent rolls down the hill. Some kind of memory stands in the wolf part of her brain. She stares off into the distance, and then down at the sand for long minutes. What is she thinking? Where do these memories take her?

Maybe in a prior life she lived in the desert, ran with the coyotes, chased down the jackrabbits for a meal. Or perhaps in a prior life she flew high above riding the winds and circling the lands below.

Luna Luckdragon fancies herself my defender, my protector. She tries to be so brave as wind makes things go thump and bang. She tries to ignore the taunt of the coyotes, the hidden scent that rides the winds of unknown scary animals. Loud noises frighten her and I undeniably become the pack leader as she hides between my legs.

I can't open the window at night. Even though the coyotes pass by in silence, Luna goes from a dead sleep to instant alert, all atwitter, full defense mode. Coyotes bother her. Fascinating and terrifying. Familiar yet strange. Friend or foe? She doesn't know. She will worry for hours until there is no trace of their sound and their scent is gone. Does she feel a kinship in any way with the desert canines? The coyote, wolves, or foxes?

She watches in curiosity as the little birds flit across the sand. Hop and stop. Brave little birds take no notice of her. She hunts the wild fly, nosing it from behind. Tracking as it rises into the air. Shaking her head with surprise and irritation as it lands on her nose.

Wind flips her ears lazily around until the sound of some animal catches her interest and she is at point again. Tense. At attention. Ready for action, but not sure what that would be. Her nose twitches and she stares into the distance, inhaling in soft puffs. Searching. Squinting into the sun. Nothing. She relaxes again. No threat.

Its Valentine's Day. No romantic interlude here. No fancy dinner or flowers. I sit in the quiet of the Mojave Desert with my faithful pup. Yes, we have escaped the rain of the Pacific Northwest and the snow that surrounds my little cabin back home for a bit. Is it just a mere change of scenery that we are enamored of? Are we in love with this place? Luna thinks so, at least in the winter.

Terry M. Mandeville

nose to the wind

nose to the wind
eyes seeking upward towards the light
she traces the birds' flight
thinking hard
pondering, reasoning
always on guard

a whisper in the distance
her ears perk
head tilts and jerks
nose twitches
inhaling the air
full of information
education
saturation

a slight scent on the breeze
a whiff
a sniff
reveals life
ripe with possibility

CHAPTER 14

SOUND TRAVELS IN THE

DESERT

quiet, music, and sound baths

Terry M. Mandeville

quiet

desert stretches unbroken to the sky
open wide
endless quiet
deafening, not a sound, not a cry

tranquility mediates
predicates
vegetates
alone, quiet penetrates
allowing a chance to mediate
to think, to feel, to hesitate

quiet, so still
not even a breeze to toss the sands and break the chill
quiet, no signs of civilization split the air
the true spirit of the earth laid bare

endless quiet broken
single chirp spoken
by desert bird trilling an omen

prowling coyotes howl
followed by yips and yowls
low growls
grow distant and silence is again allowed

"Sound travels in the desert!" the landlord cautioned me. "People are sensitive to noise and loud music. We have an agreed upon quiet time from 10 in the evening until 8 in the morning. Keep in charge of your dog. No crazy barking, alright?"

He sizes me up out of the corner of his eyes, and then shrugs. I guess he seems to think it is fairly safe with this 70-something year old woman in residence.

The desert is so still, so quiet. The dove coos to break the silence, and goes on for a while talking about his mate, and the nest they will build, and the coming spring. The wind kicks up, gentle little puffs at first. Soon it builds to stronger gusts blowing the pine needles around, shushing through the yucca, rustling the tufts on the Joshua trees.

I look out across the expanse for miles and miles. Houses nestled low, like silent little boxes. Endless earth, endless sky. When the wind shifts the right direction, you can hear for miles.

"Wooooooossssssh" the wind gusts, ebbs and flows. I listen. Voices in the wind, real or imagined? Wind can pick up unexpectedly. Fierce, blowing suddenly hard and loud. It rushes unhindered over the sand, picking up speed, whistling through the willows with a moan. Sounds like a baby crying in the night.

A coyote yips down the rise, and then quiets. The coyotes' song is complex music, the underlying howl, the staccato yips. Eerie in the night, echoing off the rocks.

Even during the quiet times there are bird cries. The hunter or hunted? Bird song. The quail's "chip-chip-chip, crear-crear" flutters on the wind. Roadrunner slurs a 5 note "co-coo-coo-coo-coooooo." The circling Red Tailed Hawk calls "kee-eeeee-arr." The doves "coo," sparrows "chirp," humming birds "hum." At night the owls hoot.

Nature is augmented by an abundance of human-made music in the desert. Concerts and music festivals at the JT saloon, Pappy and Harriet's, campgrounds, and out on the desert sand. Musicians are drawn here, and some die here. The desert is the ideal backdrop for many a music video.

Donovan Leitch ("Catch the Wind," "Colours," "Mellow Yellow") used to live in JT, on his acreage called "Rancho Mellow

Yellow." It was a colorful house built into the hills on 5 acres, surrounded by 150 acres of wildness. I tried to find Rancho Mellow Yellow today, with no luck.

At any rate, he no longer lives in JT. I often wonder if Donovan was here when he wrote "Happiness Runs" because the words about a pebble on the sand resonate so with this desert. Words all about the ancient sand. Millions of years, trillions of years of rocks crushed, weakened, ground to this white-gold and sparkly covering. These sands have beheld unwritten history, the beginnings, the origins. Did these sands witness the ancient space travelers or gods as they formed their earth for their own purposes? Did they hear the big bang echoing across the universe? Did they watch as microbes became protozoa, became sea creatures, took their first breath, formed wings and took to the air? Did they tremble as the T Rex smashed down terrible big feet; as they died and were wiped from earth and memory? Did they cry when homo sapiens waged wars, devastated the forests, wiped out whole species of animals?

I wish my old friend Dave Farcy was still alive. I remember so vividly when he taught us that song, "Happiness Runs," for a Songfest at Camp Robbinswold. If I had my guitar, would I still be able to play it? Ah well. I made a little margarita and a toast to Donovan, and Dave, and to Graham Parsons too.

Gram Parsons, of the Byrds and Flying Burrito Brothers fame, was an early pioneer in blending Country and Rock music. An outstanding guitarist and composer. He used to come to JT to "commune with nature" (IE: take lots of psychedelics, barbiturates, and drink lots of alcohol). In 1973 he OD'd and died in room #8 of the Joshua Tree Inn. Before his death, Parsons allegedly stated that he wanted his body cremated in Joshua Tree National Park and his ashes spread over Cap Rock. Despite this, Parson's stepfather had arranged to take his body to New Orleans.

To carry out Parsons' wishes, his friends stole his body from Los Angeles International Airport, borrowed a hearse, drove to Cap Rock and attempted to cremate Parsons' body by throwing five gallons of gasoline into the coffin and throwing a lit match inside. There was an enormous fireball. Unfortunately, it did not cremate his body. The result was a mess and a legal bru-ha-ha. So, I went to Cap Rock in the Park to pay my respects.

In 2016 Paul McCartney played a rare small club performance for 300 fans at Pappy and Harriet's between weekends of the historic "Desert Trip" concert in Indio. The venue's online calendar did not list any performers for the night. A recording on their answering machine said the $50 tickets (cash only) would go on sale at the box office the night of the concert starting at 6:30 PM. No one was to be allowed to line up before 3 PM. Not only McCartney, but Robert Plant, Rufus Wainwright, Leon Russell, Sean Lennon, and many others have played at Pappy and Harriet's.

One of the greatest rock records of all time is entitled "the Joshua Tree" by U2. Although the Irish rock group had not frequented JT, and the album was not recorded here, Bono had fallen in love with the deserts of the world. He was seeking a quality for the group's album that would evoke the symbolism of the "richness of spirit." Over several days the band travelled on a bus thru the Mojave Desert, photographing along highway 395 in the ghost town of Bodie, the Harmony Motel in 29, and all around Death Valley. They found the Joshua trees, with their spiritual history, to be the perfect image; an entity that survives in the desert despite all odds.

As they drove down Route 190 by Darwin, they found "the" Joshua tree, one single tree that seemed perfect. An image of the group with this tree appears on the back cover of the album. The centerfold shows the group on either side of the tree. Separate photographs were placed on each side of the sleeve. On the front cover the group was shown at Zabriskie Point in Death Valley, although different photos were used for various issues of the CD and cassettes. The lone tree used for the sleeve fell over in 2000. There is a plaque nearby that asks "have you found what you're looking for?" an allusion to a song from the album.

JT is also a mecca for sound baths. This meditative practice, where one is "bathed" in sound waves, has a worldwide history thousands of years old. Currents of soothing, deep cleansing, resonating, overlapping vibrations echoing sound from traditional crystal and metal bowls and pyramids, bells, chimes, rattles, tuning forks, wind instruments, drums, keyboards, and/or human voice lead one into a deep state of meditation and relaxation. It is meant to help with mood; to banish stress, depression, pain, anxiety, tension and fatigue. It is said to shut off the body's fight-or-flight reflex and trigger healing.

My first sound bath is conducted in a tiny house painted in neon blue with yellow butterflies way up on the hill in the middle of the desert. Lying on soft pillows, open windows let in a warm breeze that blows through fluttering gauzy curtains. Sound waves over me, a "sonic soak," waves of soothing echoing sounds. Resonating Tibetan crystal bowls, punctuated by a reed instrument and gongs pulsate. Soothing, overlapping vibrations, usher in a state of contemplation. The practitioner stands me in an enormous bowl while she makes it sing around me, and it shivers my entire body.

Later I score a spot at the gold standard of American sound baths for a group session at the Integratron in Landers. A quiet and eager group is escorted into the wooden dome and up the narrow ladder into the top portion of the structure. We all find our own mats on the floor, aligned toward a circle of 20 huge pure quartz crystal singing bowls, and settle in. After an introduction by the practitioner, we experience three quarters of an hour of harmonic sound played live. The Integratron is the only all-wood, acoustically perfect sound chamber in the USA, making possible reportedly remarkable rejuvenating sonic capabilities.

The clarity in the resonation of the bowls, combined with the acoustics of the all-wood structure, is said to have "alternative" healing powers. The theory is that sound baths have a deep relaxing and calming effect. The effects reportedly include rejuvenation, introspection, awareness, relaxation, and peace of the body and mind. Each bowl is said to be tuned to a different note that is attuned to the chakras of the body. According to the architect of the Integratron, the 50 ft. diameter parabolic dome was built atop a magnetic vortex of geometric forces that amplify energy needed for human cell rejuvenation and healing. The dome was designed to focus that energy.

I lay on my mat, eyes closed, meditating as the practitioner plays various tones on the bowls. Each tone bends the note and reverberates in ways that make it feel like it is coming in and out of my body in waves. The intensity of the sound is a deep vibration from head to toe. Some of the tones feel soothing. Others are somewhat disquieting. Each different note seems to vibrate in a different part of my body. After experiencing the hypnotic vibrations, we take a little time to recover and come back down to earth. We take turns standing and giving thanks in the center of the room. The resonance of our voices reverberates back to us.

Sound and music in the desert are ever-present, even if just the wind and the shifting sands. It is as if the music of the universe focuses here, bright and intense.

Terry M. Mandeville

sound travels in the desert

sound travels in the desert, yips and tweets
a plethora of dogs bark to greet
they warn, defend and roam unleashed
barking becomes a wave down the street
one after another they continue and repeat

across the valley

distant roar of traffic winding down to town
speeding hotrods, distant highway sound
car engine revving up as decibels pound
old beater cars with no mufflers
doing doughnuts in the sand
around and around

a door slams, some music begins
hard driving beat as my head spins
can't make out the tune or the words within

yep, sound travels in the desert

CHAPTER 15

PEOPLE WATCHING

desert rats and eccentric characters

Terry M. Mandeville

people in the desert

california girl shines
short short-shorts define
riding up a bit high
she heads up the trail, then realigns
to her cell phone confined

edmund and winston
john and don
the old folk stroll along
in the desert dawn
drawn
to see all there is before it is gone

park rangers in faded grey
marching the trails all day
familiar with the way
of the land they try to save

stoned hippie
in a sarape
happily tripping

The first peoples of the Joshua Tree area knew the abundance of the land and how to live well here. There was a feast of mesquite pods, acorns, pine nuts, and a variety of seeds, berries, fruits of the various cacti, beans, corn, and roots. They hunted the rabbits, deer, big horn sheep, reptiles, amphibians, birds, bison, wild pigs, squirrels, and other small animals.

Human beings have been in the area for eons. There are many prehistoric and historic sites of the Paleo-Natives. The earliest known inhabitants of the Joshua Tree area were the Pinto people who lived in the basin 4,000 to 8,000 years ago up until relatively recently. When the glaciers melted, the area flowed with a river and big game was plentiful. They were a nomadic people, dependent upon hunting and gathering. As the water sources became scarcer during the Pleistocene era, the Pinto people adapted for a while by hunting smaller game and gathering seeds. Eventually they moved on. There are sites with remains of their art, pottery, abodes, cow camps, roads, shelters, and tools that they left behind. Subsequent cultures lived, hunted, foraged for food, and milled seed in the area.

The park today includes 15 native tribal communities as "the original stewards of the land."

Over the centuries, the earth continued to change. Even as the landscape dried out, knowledgeable native peoples thrived in this place as a seasonal, nomadic hunting area. The land was fertile, and they appreciated its countless gifts.

The Chemehuevi called themselves Nüwüwü ("The People") or Tantáwats ("Southern Man"). They were the next known people who inhabited the Joshua Tree area of the Mojave desert. The name Chemehuevi comes from either the Mojave word meaning "those who play with fish" or a Quechan word meaning "nose in the air like a roadrunner." They were a nomadic people who came to Southern California about 400 years ago. They hunted and gathered, and built temporary small round shaped houses called "wickiups" made of willow, dirt and brush. In the winter they lived in large villages.

According to legend, the Oasis of Mara originally belonged to the Serrano people. Serrano is Spanish for "mountain dweller." They called themselves Yuhaviatam (people of the pines), Maarrênga'yam (people from Morongo), or Taaqtam (meaning just the people). They were the few who had survived the smallpox epidemic that devastated the native populations and they knew how to thrive in the hostile desert. The Cahuilla, or Ivilyuqaletem, lived in small villages near reliable water sources in the area. They ate the fruit of the fan palm, and made baskets and sandals from the leaves.

In more recent times, Bill and Frances Keys homesteaded the Desert Queen Ranch in a blind canyon inside what is now the National Park. I cannot imagine living two days by horse from the closest town. They would have to travel there for wood, gasoline, medical care, mail, anything they had to buy. No electricity at the homestead. They had to dig far down for well water but the area was also subject to quick, short flash floods. They made their own bricks from the clay and carved chunks of boulders. It was a hostile environment for growing crops and keeping animals, yet these resilient people actually succeeded. Frances Keys birthed and raised seven children there and died there in 1963 at age 75, followed by her husband Bill in 1964.

Terry M. Mandeville

Today you never know what you are going to see next in the ongoing movie of a Joshua Tree National Park trail head parking lot. Hikers, families, rock climbers; a mix of people.

A shiny red sports car speeds to a stop, exuding giggles and music. "California girls" unfold and emerge. Flawless painted faces, not a bleached blond hair out of place. Tight little short, short cutoff jeans, frayed to just the right length, riding up a bit high, sprouting long smooth crispy tan legs. Clean new sneakers in black and white, broad brimmed felted hats with chinstraps hanging low. Stylish. They shrug into their expensive, new for the occasion, tan suede knapsacks over spotless bright white blouses and head up the path a bit. Then they stop, confused, frustrated, cell phones in hand with no signal. How can they tell their friends about the torturous terrain? The sand and dirt? The sweat and toil? They turn around, back to the car and civilization.

Strong muscled legs of the Park Rangers climb out of a truck. They stretch and twist, then start up the trail in their faded grey shirts and multi-pocket khakis. Carabiners hang from dusty belt loops; they are prepared for the inevitable. Expecting, protecting, anticipating.

I wanted to be a park ranger in the Olympic National Park when I was younger. Living all year in a cabin or tent in the wilderness. Hiking the trails. Learning all about the flora and fauna. Protecting the wildlife, saving the wild for the children. No television or electricity. Campfires from damp wood. Candles and lanterns lighting pathways into the night. Cooking dehydrated and freeze-dried concoctions over a tiny camp stove. Meadows for a yard, clean rivers to drink from; trees for storage, protection, shade. Snow patches as entertainment, rocky passes as triumph. Sounded like the ideal life to me.

A psychedelically painted old Volkswagen bus chugs down the road. The driver suddenly halts, emerges, and stands in the middle of the road, apparently quite stoned. His eyes are seeing other things; not the cars passing him, nor the people walking by. Perhaps the winds are talking to him. Maybe the Yucca People are speaking wise thoughts. Maybe the UFOs are telepathically imparting the secret of immortality. His wool serape covers him brightly in the warm day and it makes me sweat just to see him so bundled up. His eyes are wide and dark beneath straight black hair. He dances there, in the road alongside the parking lot. Slow graceful moves like a ballet, mimicking tai chi with his own patterns meaningful only to him. Cars gently curve around him, not really seeming to take much notice, an ordinary occurrence in the desert. People smile, nod, and move on.

A clean older black Ford Focus pulls in, glides up slowly beside my car in the Ryan Mountain parking lot, and stops gently, patiently waiting. A handler emerges and scurries around the car. Doors are opened and three nuns unfold into the windy desert, complete with old style floor length black habits; long black tunics, black veils fluttering. It's the height of the Covid Pandemic, and so they have black masks that match their black garb. At first, I think they look out of place. Then I realize that nothing is really out of place in Joshua Tree. Just another chapter in the ongoing strange story that is this surreal desert. They move slowly, perhaps with reverence for the earth, the wonder of creation, the beauty.

They move, starting up the trail, a flash of dark stockings and sensible white tennis shoes. Gliding more than walking up the trail, they smile serenely, sure in their appreciation of God's creation. Their handler leads the way, circling and doting, protecting, respecting. Nuns in the desert. A concept so odd, so out of place, yet so comfortable. Nuns in the desert. Like any other of God's creatures, at home where their father placed them. They looked so calm, so much at peace; as if all the yoga and meditation, all the hot tubs and chamomile tea, all the valium and margaritas in the world was melded into their being.

You can hear them before they even turn into the lot. The screaming kids, the overwhelmed adults. They are crammed together in the old Ford station wagon, camping gear lashed to the roof. Engine turns off and the kids pour out, running up boulders as the adults yell after them. They run amok onto the sand, mom is not too far behind, running breathlessly and barking ignored commands.

Look up. See the little specks high up the rock face, along the crack, near the top? Wearing shorts with many pockets, gripping gloves and supple climbing boots. They are caressed by rope and harness. Tenuous toe and finger hold barely there. Beaners and pitons. Chalk. Voices call back and forth, "On belay," "Belay on." Muscles, legs shake as they tire. High reach barely achievable. Wide stance remotely stable. Again and again, one move at a time. Up.

Two cars pull up, right after each other, over the washboard of a dirt road leaving dust clouds in their wake. They spew out humans, noisy and eager, tumbling out into the parking lot, "ooooing" and "ahhhing" in awe at the scene that lay before them. Excited chattering and clattering as they pull out bags and gear. Doors slam. Seriously outfitted with well-worn and dusty backpacks. Bring lots of water. Got your map and compass? Do you know how to use them? Sunscreen? A big hat? The 10 essentials? That trail looks mighty steep and hot. Up. All trails begin by going up. Starting at a high elevation, alien beauty starts to quicken and deepen. Muscles work. Sand in the boots. Dust coating everything. Up switch backs. Pleasant views from the barren top, of valleys below and sunsets painting the sky. Then down. Knees jarring. Stumble over loose rock.

Retired folk haul an enormous spanking new RV; AC and satellite dish atop. This is a stop on their orchestrated, AAA recommended adventure. They go slow along the twists and turns of the desert road like Sunday drivers turned loose. Hitting the brakes at every scenic sight sign, they pull off and park off-center. They take a long time getting ready, tying the shoelaces snugly, visiting and complaining about the stinking outhouse, drinking water. Preparing. Finally, they begin, walking soundlessly. The pace is slow. They are saving their breath for the higher elevation.

Snowbirds have found a place in town for their winter abode, a place to park the old RV between summer forays. TV blares politics. Gnomes, pink flamingos, and little yapping dogs in the yard. Fire the barbeque! Cane and walking stick by the door. Saturday, can't miss the Farmer's Market. Stroll on toward the village, stop to greet new friends. Buy a fresh veggie or two, a knick-knack for the great-grandchild. T-shirts that say "I'm spending my children's inheritance." Dry heat begins to warm new hips and heal as they walk off their rehab. Repaired hearts happily pump away.

the hiker

underfoot loose sand
he ambles across the land
between the rocks, cacti, and willow stands

clouds part, the coolness blasting to heat
in a heartbeat
sweat rolls down his face, blisters form on his feet

surveying the route
desert stretches out
nothing but flat and dry about

scrub oak and mojave yucca
suck the meager moisture
flies scramble for succor

the desert makes its own milieu
raw survival of the few
who brave the climb and push on through

on the outline atop the hill
tiny figures slowly mill
on top of the world, chilled, thrilled

Terry M. Mandeville

desert rat haikus

natives knew secrets
they thrived on desert richness
hidden treasures teem

europeans came
forced their ways, stole the children
eminent domain

miners had hard lives
digging for copper and gold
got rich or went bust

white homesteaders came
spread out on the desert lands
wide open spaces

jackrabbit hovels
five acres, just five dollars
no water nearby

soldiers play war games
gunfire and blasts disturb
the silent desert

CHAPTER 16

THE SKY

horizons, rocks, sunsets, sunrises and
blue forever

Terry M. Mandeville

night parts

night parts keenly
cleanly to this burgeoning morning light
sun rises to hues of pink and blue below
frigid winter night turns to a glow
blush of warmth to come
hint of the day begun

rock face shows dark teaming
brooding colors beaming
in coffee and cream, the hills seem new

the day slinks on by
bleak sun takes its place awhile in winter sky
holds for a bit on high
then sinks slowly

pale pink begins on edges bright
taking a bite out of the clouds
purple and orange hues
right against the blues

then it all dims
comes the night again

The sky may be the most astonishing thing about the Joshua Tree area. Wide above the open desert. Sunrises and sunsets are unbelievable with ever-changing color. The moon moves through various shades of gold and silver. Stars sparkle, scattered across a field of night.

The dog stirs, wakes me with a lick. Outside dark sky has just begun to lighten a bit to a slight dawning of day to come. Shimmer of gold along the outline of the hills, quickly winking to yellows, pinks and oranges reaching out and grabbing the sky. Like someone pressed fast forward, florescent vivid bands of magenta begin to glow. Then deep velvet red spreads over the horizon. Spreads outward, tie-dyeing the umbrella overhead. The final flush, the fanfare, flourishes gawdy crimson and then fades again to muted orange glow. Full sunlight enters the window, bright in the early morning.

The sun parks there, sheds more light, disguising the dark. Above high clouds spit out a silent jet trail. People in the airplanes look down from the heavens, seeing only patchwork browns, missing the details, the graceful beauty, no inkling of the tranquil below.

The desert winter sky is endless blue, rippled with strings of white to pearl grey like seashore sand. Rolling puffy white cotton occasionally drifts lazily across the sky and momentarily hides the sun. It is only temporary. The clear sky holds in no heat in winter. The wind is icy, my fingers are frozen and I pull my hood over my sniveling head. Later dark clouds roll in. Roiling deep black monsters creeping from the mountains.

One quickly notices that unbelievable rock structures in this desert are as equally awe-inspiring as the twisted Joshua tree. Ancient rock formations loom large on the horizon, jutting toward the sky. Some of them are billions of years old. The simple hand of nature has created patterns of artistic design, sometimes haphazard. Mystifying. Ready to be shaken loose. Toppling, teetering, solidifying. Light and dark combine.

Spires, domes and crags form the spine at the horizon. Distant silhouettes hide behind. Over the millennia water has trickled into the granite. The water came in contact with different chemicals and minerals inside the rock, reacted and formed clay. The soft clay eroded and rounded out large amounts of rock in strange ways.

There are caves and box canyons to explore. I could gaze, mesmerized, for hours. It's not just rocks. It is art, it is architecture. They seem sculpted with purpose, not by puny human-kind. Sculpted by the bubbly volcanic forces, tremors, quakes and upheaval. Rounded and smoothed by wind, sand, and water. Bleached by the sun. Stacked artistically atop one another. Rough like sand paper, stucco, wind pitted, grainy. Smooth like marble walls, shiny like glass. Nature's sculpture gradually chiseled through the eons.

In the desert there are no rivers to carry off rock debris, so eroded rock sticks around leaving rounded boulders and islands of rock. Picasso from strange perspectives, sensuous curves, sharp lines, odd straight angles, pockets.

Aligning columns, stacked blocks, jagged and smooth. Slabs, holes, caves. Boulders that seem as if they are falling, rolling. Layered in depth.

Somehow a tree takes hold, clings to the face. Somehow roots tunnel, find a way to water, to food, to life. Somehow the tree thrives, stays alive and reaches toward the sun.

I see shapes and figures in the rock. A man facing the sunset. Sumo wrestler hunkered, ready to tackle. Bear rubbing up a tree. Sleeping dog head resting on paws. All masterpieces.

Rocks are hard, impenetrable, and yet time has somehow sculpted them. Here are patches of metal rusted, reaching, staining. Here is bare white, bleached by sun. Here is the black of lichens, mosses, long dead and dry, now smooth and velvet.

The view is infinite, stretching out in all directions. Pristine, bold. The horizon is etched in browns and golds against canvas of blue. As the sun sets the windows of the houses below are lined in a glittering glow, reflections of a perfect day.

Desert sunsets in JT are stunning, to say the least. I have become spoiled night after night with a variety of colors and shades. The sun has been bright all day. The deep green of Joshua tree and cacti bloom are alive. Enough wind to fan away any heat. Clouds move in now, streaks and billows as the sun imperceptibly starts to lower, sometimes barely visible to the eye. It shoots rays of yellows, muted oranges. Sudden strips of fluffy soft white with pink edges like pink cotton candy layered with desert blue. Ribbons or orange begin on the horizon silhouetting irregular peaks. Now deep blood red whips behind the rocks between the pale blue. Fiery gold as the last circle of sun sinks behind the hills. It opens further with raspberry pudding blossoms across the land, the desert sun sinking behind the hills creates a deep rose glow in the sky with reds and yellows. Purples and violets as it begins to mellow. Darkening now to chili pepper red before the darkness falls altogether, like a curtain speckled with diamonds.

Now it is dark. I climb the rise by my little house, see the lights of the village below. No sound, no traffic, no streetlights. Just true peace and quiet. Looking out on the sand I can see for miles across the desert. Across treeless open terrain. Across roads and towns. Peaceful moonscape. Twisted trees that aren't really trees. Needled cactus waiting to attack. Howls of coyote, followed by chattering yips, and then the confused barking of Luna who just wants to go play.

Houses along the highway shine brightly in the night. Civilization. Lights ablaze, to push back the fear that hides in darkness. Every light shines beside a life. Sparkly, twinkling, shimmering in the night air. Like the stars above, like twinkling holiday lights, the lights of town spread out below; tumbling across the land, thrown among the rises. Between the sand and dust. Jewels in the desert.

I imagine the people there. Human abodes lit up. Shelter from the wild. Houses with children playing and laughing, together inside their fancy cave. Warm places to be on a cold desert night. Order and safely out of the dangerous chaos that abounds in the wide-open desert. Shops alight with people shopping. Restaurants alive with aroma and tasty morsels. Beer at the brewery, pizza at Sky High, music at the saloon, buying tequila at Sam's Market.

A necklace of headlights spirals before me, threading down the curves from the park. Down the hill and off into the distance. Snaking like a jeweled waterfall; winding, wavering, wandering. Up and down, curving around to the horizon, and farther. Headlights that beam into the night. Our house lights the hillside, only a speck in the grand scheme of things. Night lights outshine the stars. Create a little universe of man-made reality. The illusion of permanence, of forever.

The other night there was a full moon, rising before last light. It was unspectacular at first glance. As the sky darkened it glowed anew, grew brighter and shined in full glory. The next night the moon had a ring around it. I thought it meant that it might snow. Isn't that the associated folklore? Nonetheless, it hasn't snowed. Snow in the desert is magical. It might, we'll see.

When there is no moon, the stars are blindingly bright overhead. The Milky Way a wide swath of silver across the black. Each point of light twinkles. It is difficult to assess the shape, the borders of each individual star. Some seem to be made up of glimmers of reds and golds. I squint. Look with one eye, then the other, just to try and get a clearer vision of these celestial lights.

When the moon sets Orion is enmeshed in a billion little pinpricks of light. Like an intricate pattern in lace. Rising early, the Greek hunter Orion lights the night in the clear sky. He stands next to the river Eridanus with his two hunting dogs Canis Major and Canis Minor. He fights Taurus the bull and hunts Lepus the hare. A billion stars, like jewels, light his background. He watches, as he has for billions of years. So bright in the winter desert sky that I almost have to shield my eyes. Orion of my ancestors. Orion of my descendants. Ancient and omnipotent. Your belt, your sword, ready for battle to save human kind. You twinkle and sparkle in the dark.

I connect other dots I see in the sky. To the right of Orion, I see the big dipper. Or is it a plough? A wagon? A bucket? A saucepan? A bear? A ladle? A net? A boat? A lobster? Different cultures throughout history have gazed upon this basic design and dreamed. It points to the north star so I will never get lost on a clear night.

The night is not windy and I decide to have a campfire. Crackle of the wood burning in the night, bright flame rising upward giving light. Above the stars are bright as there is no moon tonight. Glowing coals cast shadows. There is no wind to blow the encircling willows. Peaceful stillness reigns. Calm moments, heavy with contentment unrestrained.

Terry M. Mandeville

The Constellations

When the Navajo Fire God placed the stars and constellations into the sky, they became alive. What we call the Big Dipper is really "The Bear." He hibernates in the winter, hidden from view of the night sky. As winter begins to come to an end, Bear begins to poke his head out to see if it is spring yet. By spring, Bear is anxious to begin his reign of the night sky. He leaves his winter den, and every night comes out a little more, rising higher in the sky. He always keeps his eye on the North Star to find his way home.

In the late spring Bear is spotted by three hunters, the three red stars. They chase him across the sky, still higher and higher, matching his pace. As summer begins Bear runs across the sky, still followed by the hunters. As the summer ends Bear is getting tired and heads for his home. As fall comes the hunters shoot their arrows at bear and hit him. His blood falls on the trees and turns the leaves red as he, bleeding, heads back down to his cave below the earth again to rest and regain his strength.

CHAPTER 17
ALL GOOD THINGS

hasta luego joshua tree

Terry M. Mandeville

come on home

come on home
but where is home?
everything changes
new places, new faces as i roam

i miss friends and family
familiar haunting grounds
the sounds
wind blowing through the trees
green grass and cool moist breeze

i even miss the lake icing over
pristine snow on the trees
slush covering the steep driveway
the raw frigid breeze

so, i guess my little house on the lake
is where i call my home
regardless of the changes
or where i winter or roam

Journal Of An Old Hippie Chick In The Desert

Desert rat or river otter?

While I am here in the desert, I am relatively dry and warm, while back home its cold. It's been flooding. Rivers have swollen, creeping across the streets leading north and south, and flooding the access to the bridges. The town has almost become an island of squishy mud and rivulets. Higher up at my cabin they say it is snowing again. Residents park their cars at the top of their steep driveways so they can get out if it gets deep. If it lasts too long the plows will eventually come by. It will probably melt before that.

I miss the concerts in McCormick Park, dinner at the Grange, wine tasting at William Grassie. I miss the native cutthroat leaping in the center of the lake where the ice hasn't formed, the otter hiding under the dock from the coming storms. I miss the tail slap of the beaver and the train whistle of the Empire Builder that can be heard all the way from Monroe on its daily journey. I miss the hum of the Anna's Hummingbirds and the hawks that cry out. I miss the geese and swans of winter. I miss the deer coming down to feed on bare twigs and last spring's salal leaves.

You can always come on home. As I get older, I ask myself just where is "home?" Old friends are gone, my mother and father have long passed. The house I grew up in is changed, unrecognizable. The neighborhood I grew up in has an entirely different identity than in the old days.

Where is home? I bought the little old house where we raised our kids decades ago. In the beginning it lay amid orchards, fields and farms. Now it stands small and ragged amid fancy wall-to-wall mansions. That house we sold; it was falling apart anyway. They will tear it down and build three enormous houses in its place.

Where is home? I guess home feels strongest in my little house on the lake. I will return to late winter, as it goes toward early spring. I will return to my base camp full of mushy long dead fall leaves, hills that blend stark grey, soppy moss dripping from the trees.

The wet slimy grey of winter still hovers. It will morph to another stage soon. The cycle persists, consisting of steps through the mist. Of time. Soon the muddy puddles will dry a bit, sprouting grass will grow high, bathing my world in the first spring greens. Soon sunny dandelions show their heads. Bare cherry trees will begin to bud green and blossom late winter. Early spring they sing then wink open. Pink and white petals blanket the scene like snow. Hints of pale green in the hills. Are those bare branches finally budding? No doubt as they unfold merrily to leafy shades of all manner of green.

As I approach home, unbidden, the scent of the cool moist air assaults me, followed by the rich fragrance of cedar. Damp and dank, the primal olfactory memory sinks deep into my core, soothing in familiarity, calming perfume of protection. The taste of pure cold water. I had forgotten all the rich colors of green.

I guess Joshua Tree has kind of become my home too.

Why? Why journey down to the desert? What do I get from it? What have I learned? How have I grown? Have I found the meaning of life? The meaning of death? What do I take home with me?

I do seem to have brought a renewed sense of peace home. An appreciation for my surroundings. I take away desert sand - in my pockets, my sleeping bag, the floor mats of my truck. I bring home words, thoughts and scribblings. I have leftover sun that shines within my essence. I carry the image of snowstorms in the desert, the stationary dance of the Joshua tree, the humor of Sinawava, the music of the spheres, the taste of parched surroundings ...and a pregnant kangaroo rat.

I am thinking that I will return each winter to my home in the desert, as life allows. I will know the routine of migration, like the Costa's Hummingbird.

little girl in the desert

little girl in the desert
take it slow
so you will truly know
the intimacy
the character
of the land

she breathes the dry clear air
the perfume of the life there
deep into her lungs
and holds it
deep into her soul

she looks up into the clear blueness
deep
forever out into the cosmos

she opens her eyes to see
to be
is it illusion or reality?

BIOGRAPHY

Terry Mandeville grew up and lives still in the pacific northwest. She has been writing almost all her life, appreciating the feel of words and their magical ways, their cathartic and healing capacity.

Now retired from being a nurse, her sons grown, she has time to once again explore the words locked in her head and heart.

Made in the USA
Columbia, SC
06 June 2024

36645164R00157